SALAMANDER SUN
& OTHER POEMS

Pia Tafdrup was born in 1952 in Copenhagen. She has published over 20 books in Danish since her first collection appeared in 1981, and her work has been translated into many languages. Her fourth collection, *Spring Tide*, was published in English by Forest in 1989. In 1991 she published a celebrated statement of her poetics, *Walking Over Water*. She received the 1999 Nordic Council Literature Prize – Scandinavia's most prestigious literary award – for *Queen's Gate*, which was published in David McDuff's English translation by Bloodaxe Books in 2001. Also in 2001, she was appointed a Knight of the Order of Dannebrog, and in 2006 she received the Nordic Prize from the Swedish Academy. In 2009 she won the international Ján Smrek Prize (awarded to non-Slovak, foreign poets) for her poetry.

The latest work of hers to be translated into English is *Salamander Sun and other poems* (Bloodaxe Books, 2015), combining two recent books, *The Migrant Bird's Compass* and *Salamander Sun*, which comprise the third and fourth parts of *The Salamander Quartet*. Written over ten years, its first two parts are *The Whales in Paris* (2002) and *Tarkovsky's Horses* (2006), published in English by Bloodaxe in 2010 as *Tarkovsky's Horses and other poems*. All her Bloodaxe titles are translated by David McDuff.

Pia Tafdrup's website: www.tafdrup.com

David McDuff (*b*. 1945) is a British translator of Nordic and Russian literature. His translations of Nordic and Scandinavian poetry have been published by Bloodaxe for more than thirty years. In 2013 he received the Finnish State Award for Foreign Translators.

PIA TAFDRUP

Salamander Sun

& OTHER POEMS

TRANSLATED BY
DAVID McDUFF

BLOODAXE BOOKS

Copyright © Pia Tafdrup & Gyldendal, Copenhagen 2010
(The Migrant Bird's Compass), 2012 (Salamander Sun).
Published by agreement with Gyldendal Group Agency.
Translation copyright © David McDuff 2015.

ISBN: 978 1 78037 150 4

First published 2015 by
Bloodaxe Books Ltd,
Eastburn,
South Park,
Hexham,
Northumberland NE46 1BS.

www.bloodaxebooks.com
For further information about Bloodaxe titles
please visit our website or write to
the above address for a catalogue.

Supported using public funding by
**ARTS COUNCIL
ENGLAND**

DANISH ARTS FOUNDATION

Thanks are due to the Danish Arts Foundation for providing
a grant towards translation costs for this edition.

Cover design: Neil Astley & Pamela Robertson-Pearce.

Printed in Great Britain by Bell & Bain Limited, Glasgow, Scotland, on
acid-free paper sourced from mills with FSC chain of custody certification.

ACKNOWLEDGEMENTS

The Whales in Paris (Hvalerne i Paris, Gyldendal, 2002), *Tarkovsky's Horses* (Tarkovskijs heste, Gyldendal, 2006), *The Migrant Bird's Compass* (Trækfuglens kompas, Gyldendal, 2010) and *Salamander Sun* (Salamandersol, Gyldendal, 2012) form a quartet around the four elements.

The first two parts of the quartet are published by Bloodaxe as *Tarkovsky's Horses & other poems* (2010), the second two parts as *Salamander Sun & other poems* (2015).

Some of these translations were first published in *World Literature Today, Poem, Absinthe, Plume Poetry* and *Ice Floe*.

CONTENTS

THE MIGRANT BIRD'S COMPASS

I

THE MIGRANT BIRD'S COMPASS

'Oh, travel, travel!' That is the happiest lot! And therefore we all travel: everything in the whole universe travels! Even the poorest man possesses thought's wingèd horse, and when it grows old and weak, Death takes him along on the journey, the great journey we all make. The waves roll from coast to coast; the clouds sail along the great sky and the bird flies over field and meadow. We all travel, even the dead in their silent graves fly with the Earth around the Sun. Yes, 'travel', it is an idée fixe of the whole Universe, but we men are children, we would play at 'travelling', even in the midst of the great natural journey that is made by ourselves and by things.

HANS CHRISTIAN ANDERSEN

I

Leaving Home
A reply to Lawrence Ferlinghetti's 'Autobiography'

I looked *away* from home,
on the farm which my parents
couldn't leave because
it was either the season
for sowing or harvesting
or harrowing or rolling,
    an outlying farm
standing solitary
on the fields
between two small villages.
At night I sometimes dreamt
that I could fly
over the trees
on wings constructed
from branches or other
available material,
        but always woke up
on the earth.
I disembarked
on foreign shores
in the books I borrowed
in the book bus
where the evening light fell in,
making the gilded letters
on the spines of the books shine
and the safe, good smell
of earlier readers
that clung to the pages
            struck me in greeting.
I rowed the last part of the way
to an island
in the small lake in the garden, encouraged
by my mother's mother,
        who read *Robinson Crusoe* to me.
I established a prairie life
out on the fields,
when they were harvested,
and the sheaves
could be stacked

15

into forts I knew
from cowboy films
on long Sunday afternoons
with my male cousins.
Or after School Cinema I continued
David Livingstone's expedition
into the heart of Africa
equipped
with machete and compass
in between the beech trees
in the dark place right at the bottom of the garden
and dug myself
Eskimo-like
into holes in the snow
to sit absolutely still, listening
in the creaking winter
to what even back then
had vanished
        and would not come back.
I dived straight down
into the Stone Age
after history hour was over,
ate berries and nuts
and ground
handfuls of my father's
newly harvested barley between two stones
round by the old chicken coop,
where foxes
dug in under the fence.
With the gardener's children I played
at travelling circuses,
in my bathing suit walked on a tightrope
stretched between the trees,
after a visit
by Circus Benneweis.
I started an Egyptian collection
at home
in my own room
after a tour of the Glyptotek art museum
with my grandfather,
who guided the way from the earliest times
up to the Roman emperors
and as a souvenir

gave me
a plaster cast
of an Egyptian scribe,
                    which still
stands on my window sill –
as my father
on a lathe in the workshop
kept meteors fallen
black-seething
on his fields, magical
lava-like stones,
sent straight
from the universe to
                    him.
I listened
to birds that flew
from exotic lands
to settle
in the bushes of *our* garden.
I would not have gone anywhere,
if my aunt had not
kidnapped my sister and me
and hidden us
one afternoon in the half-darkness
of Kronborg's casemates.
Or if my grandmother and grandfather,
when my brother
had been born,
and my mother for a time lost
sight of my sister and me,
had not abducted us
for a weekend to Arild,
on the other side of Øresund,
which I often looked out across
as I hung about at Langebro
in Hellebæk
and in all weathers watched
the world pass by, with
                    only one desire:
to take part in it,
there, where things happened,
    but here
for the first time as a ten-year-old

17

in a new country
was confronted
by rocks
that could be climbed,
a journey that had an effect
like an injection of dreams
and drove me
later to try
            to leave home.
No one
must hold on to me,
no one
must put obstacles in the way,
I was willing
to run the risk
            life is.
I left the farm one day in anger,
packed
my clothes in a bundle
set off,
as I had seen
vagabonds portrayed,
to walk around the Earth,
or at least
– as perhaps was hoped –
far out on the field
in the direction of
the village that lay further off,
   was fetched back
by my father.
Yet only for a time,
for I soon invented a code,
                  a new alphabet,
which galloping
led me away
across the empty paper,
   so scarily white
that not even an angel had left its trace.

II

THE ELEMENT OF MOTION

The Road Anyone Can Go

I go led by sleepless nerve paths
   in front of my shadow,
cross dense traffic, find
a passable path,
go right, left,
traverse bridges over streams
and fords,
reach a track I want to follow.
The straight road is not
   the shortest.
The air is chill and raw, the landscape
is lit by the earliest morning sun,
cold and warmth sprout up
at the same time.
Now it is now I go
enticed by dreams
   to which birds migrate.
Notice a sharp tang of plants
that once grew,
hear sounds purring
of *before*.
   What does the road want of me?
Look out across the wide-stretched terrain
with its network of scents and false scents.
The fear
is always there,
      thus a pupil opens.
The road changes pace, keeps me awake –
I branch, collect myself
mark
on the map of the future
   a route
bound for uncertainty.

Dark October

Cross a strait
in a boat at night
   like my mother.
Cross a strait
at night in another cutter
   like my father.
Flee like growing crowds
                     of displaced persons.
The black water
       is open.
My mother without luggage, but wearing
layer upon layer of clothes,
crammed into the hold among many others,
down against her mother and sister
   with a hat to throw up in.
The order is for dead
silence
     until the boat is out of the harbour.
On the deck in the pitch darkness
my mother's father follows the voyage
to Swedish territory in heavy seas,
lashed to the mast
so as not to fall overboard.
No German patrols, only tugboats.
The black water
       is open.
Relatives are left behind –
friends   houses   belongings   a beloved country.
Cross a strait
on a dark October night
with a fisherman and crew
who don't know the exact route.
Try to find port
by sounding the depths,
try to find port with signals
from searchlights' glare.
At last dock at the right berth in Höganäs
shouted in by Swedish soldiers.

21

A way across the water   homecoming
with no home
              to what future?
Not to flee from oneself,
    but so as to be allowed to be oneself.

In the Mountain Cavern

Far in the northern Apennines,
a grotto hall of marble, a pressure
from all sides as if under water, as if sunk
deeper
    than deep.
Forehead, scalp, temple,
the cranium's tectonic plates
grate and creak,
        small avalanches happen –
the head is on the point of exploding.
Time bites
     its own tail.
The night sky everywhere
the night sky's rumbling spasms
   in silent ringing
between the cavern's floor, ceiling and walls.
Remember, stretched in a wave
between pain and vertigo,
in a *flash*
  my life as a foetus.
The massive force
        and only one bawling way OUT
                to miles-wide, snow-blind happiness.

23

The Last Journey

'The last journey', it's called,
though the destination
has no name –
but in language's shadow exists
a permeable place
where my father
          passes through
and still *is* with us.
Whatever country I'm in
   I meet him
as what is written
between the lines,
   meet him
equally calm, equally present.
He knows
where I am,
          shows up
with a chieftain's dignity.
My mother still casts nets
with her words, says 'we'
and 'our' house,
   even though he has long been dead.
Perhaps one is
born
to take part in the infinite.

First Flight

From the beach and up into the air
I received my first flight,
                    carried on my stomach
by my father's feet,
which were about as long
as my body back then.
I hung in the warm wind
between the buzz of insects
and the scream of gulls.
Down there was seen from up here –
my father on his back in the sand
    I in the sky,
my father below
    I up above
balancing on the soles of his feet
between the wings of the birds
                    in a white sucking.
Waves beat numbingly
in on the shore, salt
bit into the skin.
I flew by a route that led away,
    where tomorrow begins.
Cloud after cloud sailed towards me,
    I floated
out beyond the body's limits,
looked down at my father,
the pilot, who controlled the direction,
circled in the blood mist
of a moment,
landed again on the warm sand,
    securely
back on his planet, from which
years later I went out into the world
while space opened
                    in a dreamed echo.

The Road Is Alive

Armies of people, animals
and vehicles
    move the road's course.
Tracks are stamped on the verge
in the same direction
around the soggy dough.
More people, more cattle
in rain, sleet and snow
    for miles.
Wheels plough their way in the wilderness
in mud, in mire,
in winds that flay
the clouds in the sky.
Side by side
run roads of earth and sand
together with the fiction
                of other traces.
Foot, paw, hoof...
Animals and people appear
and disappear, the earth
swallows bone fragments,
drinks the blood.
Passable lanes are formed, others grow over,
    routes are displaced
as people walking and driving
through centuries
        don't meet –
but no place along the whole distance
avoids those
    who have passed.
Shadows
are cast over shadows
on a road populated by destinies.
Assaults, lootings, axe-blows
                before the blessing.

International Airspace

Before anyone, with the strength of falling lightning,
focused on terrorists,
   my grandmother and I stood
on a landing in Copenhagen Airport
at windows that faced the aeroplane parking ramp
and waved goodbye
          to my mother's father.
Downstairs in the transit hall
we followed unhindered
an anthill of passengers.
From there one had access
to the entire globe,
        and up rose
dreams from every land.
My grandmother pointed to the sky:
– *Here you see international airspace.*
Cows, pigs and horses
had to be tended on my parents' farm.
I had not been beyond
Denmark's borders,
I wasn't going
      to take wing
like the people who swarmed around in the hall,
but understood that journeys
to anywhere at all
   had their beginning there.
I waved to my grandfather, whose hat
drowned
in the mass of hats on their way up into the plane.
Further away lay
runways for take-off and landing.
Planes rose noisily into the air, disappeared
in the distance. Others
landed on the concrete
to glide in towards a gate.
An ocean of dread blended
with another of happiness –
flowed into dizzying drops,
when I looked up to what was the sky,
but now revealed itself
          as international airspace.

27

Travel Light

By all means take my suitcase, which now again
is too heavy to carry – packed with
nightdress, piles of underwear and socks,
dresses, skirts, belts,
blouses with short and long sleeves,
sweaters, jerseys, long pants,
thermal or swimwear, shoes
for walking, running, shoes
for dresses, trousers, boots, sandals,
toiletries for almost any
conceivable situation,
umbrella, sun hat, sunscreen
(high factor), lip balm
(also high factor), reading
for changing moods,
matches, candles, address list,
alarm clock (though the phone has an alarm),
water heater, favourite tea, travel mug,
hairbrush, hair dryer, hair spray,
jacket, hat, gloves, scarves,
   all carefully stacked
like the words here, in order to give
at least an illusion of order.
And for special expeditions:
drops, sterile syringes,
chlorhexidine, plaster, paraghurt,
penicillin, sulfa tablets,
imodium, milk of magnesia,
mosquito balsam, mosquito spray, iodine…
Not to mention the hand luggage
with the *most* indispensable items:
Passport, tickets, money, travel insurance,
reading glasses, mobile phone, computer,
phrasebook, map, compass, diary,
notebooks, paper, pen, mechanical pencils,
camera, adapter, possible special medications,
toothbrush, makeup and extra clothes
   for if the suitcase is delayed or lost.
I have packed for tomorrow –
but yesterday travels back with me in a mess

of dusty shoes, broken shoelaces, the clothes
with dirt and stains,
strange, indefinable odours, immediately
registered by the cat,
   and gifts that must be unwrapped carefully.

Amulet

Whether someone once stole it
from an art museum's collection
   can only be guessed,
but for the first trip across the Atlantic
a friend with fear of flying gave me
                                 a black amulet
which I hung on a chain around my neck.
Since then
I have made no journey
without this amulet,
          a small stone seal
with an engraved image
of an Egyptian man,
used as a signature
by illiterates...
How it would have gone
   without an amulet
I hardly dare to think,
   but with
that Egyptian man from another millennium
I have visited many countries
and, edified, left as many
again
like the well that absorbs the light to itself,
   one dream richer.
Shrewdly he has marked out
the right course, warned
against dangers –
watched over me in every way.
No better traveling companion
could have taken the responsibility for irresponsibility.

30

On Motorbike in Nightdress

On motorbike in nightdress
down Fredensborg High Street.
My parents
were far away, and I
   immune to sleep, tempted
to the point of trembling in every fibre
by one of the hands on the farm
   to sit on his motorbike.
I balanced behind him, clung
tight about his waist, as if
on the back of a horse
being brought home from the pen,
I were throwing my arms around its neck.
…Remember the earth and the clouds,
the sky with a colour
           I had not seen before,
the road, the speed and the word
   'horsepower',
that a summer night could be
so different from any bedtime story.
…Remember the ride as we hurtled past
butcher, baker, bank
and greengrocer,
the roar
of the machine between the houses,
the wind that stripped my arms
the thrill of an unfamiliar adult world.
…Remember the vibration as it spread
                       oceanic
from lap and up back and neck,
to the head. My cheek
pressed in against the farmhand's back.
I didn't wait for that evening's story,
my hair drank of the wind,
               I lived it.

Transport

Carry water
in a sieve,
transport it onward
in jars with no bottom,
serve it in bowls,
from where it evaporates.
Drink of it here
in great gulps,
          ceaselessly –

Stumbling Stone

Not a stone in the shoe,
that chafes long before
it registers as stone,
but a stone on the road,
                    a stumbling stone,
that suddenly makes the heart
pound in the chest as waves
roll from foreign shores
   in towards the coast,
where I grew up,
   into the poems I write.
A stone
between before and after
at an insurmountable distance
on a hot day
without a cloud in the sky.
A stone,
lying as it does,
   sun up there,
   stone down here,
substance, matter,
in order to point out
that I am scarcely
on the road –
but that the mind is racing.
What does a person think of
   while walking?
Not necessarily of travel,
the legs walk by themselves,
once they have learned
   to walk.
Quite often the person thinks about
 not having much time
              to live,
thinks about events that are
like scars in the heart
or about changing
for the better, at least
   trying.

33

I walk on the road
the mind is racing
        over a wayless terrain,
                far beyond this moment.

Signpost

The world was old
even before
it was born,
for no one learns
from others' experience,
   only by making
the mistakes oneself
over and over again.
Atlas, globe, map,
the world *was* discovered,
   only not by me...
In the heart is
the signpost
   I follow.
What else can I
navigate by
so exactly?

Staying the Night

Remove shoes and quickly strip off clothes
in a chill room
with windows facing out onto a wall,
    drained after the day's job.
Slacks, blouse, socks, panties and bra,
unfasten buckles, unbutton, unhook –
throw some things on a battered chair,
    let the rest drop
to the floor.
Lie down in the allotted bed with echo
of strangers before me, bodies
    that smell of rain and moonlight.
Crawl in under the duvet
in the only vacant guesthouse
draw my knees up under me,
curve my body
            into a circle,
delve down into an archaeological night,
    with ear against the pillow intercept
a continuous murmur from lodgers
in a whirl
        backwards in time,
at last let oneself be licked in the face
by sleep.
Be woken, first by lustful moaning
on the other side of the wall,
later by shouts and footsteps in the hallway,
doors slamming open and shut.
Almost reluctantly
            straighten oneself out to adult size.
Get up for a new job in a new place,
try to focus
on the face in the mirror's icy light
    without holding judgment day.
Find maps and check departure times,
gather one's belongings,
                one's sadness or one's joy.

Over Field and Meadow

From the meadows the mist rises dense
between horses with horse-cloths and cows
in the dewy grass.
The mist penetrates across the fields,
  swirls diffusely above the road.
The stippled lines sew us out
through the white vapour.
A bus full of people
in shared dozing up the hills
and down them in soft curves.
Light
glimpsed from scattered houses
and secluded farms.
In a muted vision dogs are let out
  as after a long winter.
The tender green gleam
of winter corn in the blackness,
                    the silence
in sleeping maize fields from last year.
Windmills fetch the day in,
the morning mist disperses
  mile by mile.
An ever greater segment of the world
is reflected in the eye,
birds
  fly with us in the air.
Last stop is the railway station,
I prepare
to get off. Sound
is back like barbs
that toxic fasten, the day
hardly distinguishable from days
where none of us look as if
we are going to die
                of love.

Which Direction?

I could have belonged
to a flock, a shoal,
a buzzing swarm,
but I AM alone.
I doubt, uncertainly
   I make
a choice. At the same second
                 the cut occurs.
I do not have the same opportunities
as a bisected earthworm
whose two parts each seek their direction.

Picnic, a Prelude

If my grandmother had become an architect,
which as a young bricklayer's apprentice she
aspired to be,
until my grandfather got other plans
for her future
within the four walls of the home,
     Copenhagen would have
been a different city today
and 'architect' more
than a capsized word in her mouth.
     If my mother had been employed
as a receptionist at the desk
of Hotel Trouville in Hornbæk,
guests from all over the world would have
received the best service,
     which did not happen,
because my father found a better solution,
                              a brand-new baby
that would be cared for
within the four wings of the farmhouse.
– *'Is home not good enough for you, then?'*
     Letters from my mother reached me
in a straight bird-line –
no matter how many wing-beats, I was gone.
Thus
I felt at home
wherever I arrived.
White envelopes with her
unmistakable, circular handwriting
     scrutinised and deciphered in many lands,
letters about my brother, my father and sister
and all her cats
'Your father has sowed the field to the east
and I have been to the hairdresser's.'
I slit the letters open
                    and out poured the sun.
Yet – *'Take me with you,'*
they said, between the lines
to me who was off to see
     how other people lived,

39

see icebergs in Greenland, nose about
in Hanoi's little shops, send out my tentacles
in Bogota, confront myself
with Australia's wildlife
but quite often encounter
beggars, robbers, swindlers and those
who were worse, men who asked:
– *'Do you want to get married?'*
I said no, because I was married,
    at least on paper.
– *'What are you doing here, then?*
Go home and look after your children!'
    How could people in other cultures
understand my desire to travel?
What was I doing in the West Bank?
Or why was it important
to cross Chicago's no-man's-land?
    Who has had a grandmother
who taught one to travel
in spite of fever, at that?
    A picnic was cancelled because I was ill,
instead, with my sister and me
she wandered up and down
the moss-green carpet in the passage, told us
of all the gnarled trees in the woods,
of the mushrooms we were going to pick,
until at last we
flopped down with the filled basket
                    and had a picnic in the greenness.

No Admittance

PRIVATE it said on the sign
but I *had to* anyway,
ever since I could read, go
along the private road, bathe
on the private beach, swim
in the private lake, until an owner
drove me away with threats.
I *had to* trespass
    not in order to invade,
but to understand
what it was I was not allowed
to have a share in...
For every fence a high jump
or a climb is enough.
At every barrier there is
a solution.
    Adam and Eve ate
    of a very private tree,
so why not taste the plantation owner's
most tempting variety?
Why not read
other people's letters and diaries,
whose content was hardly distinguishable
                        from my own life,
but suddenly opened
like the sky
when it shakes the lightning from itself.
Why not take a look inside
on the private shelf in my mother's closet.
    What lay in wait for me?
Why not pull out drawers
in bureau and desk, examine
boxes in the loft? For here was
what was not talked about.
Cross the line
            in order to obtain INSIGHT
                        and feel SHAME
                        at the same time.
I don't lack imagination,
that is not why

I am enticed.
In the same way as what is whispered
is more interesting than what is shouted,
I want to find out
what is behind the sign
with the inscription PRIVATE.
Quite often the conclusion is:
Here the strongest feelings are concealed,
here is enacted the drama
                              a life is,
here the diary entry smells
                              of skin.
The lifeblood is what one seeks
in the diaries of Hans Christian Andersen,
of Strindberg, of Kafka
and many others who wrote
for themselves,
but still wanted to bring the hidden
                              out into the light.
This is the Earth
and I want to know it –
when a warning blocks the way,
I want to be like the wind
                              without limit.
Nothing shall hinder me, certainly not a sign.

Thought's Wingèd Horse

Thoughts find their way
forward in a steady flow,
    in leaps, in zigzags.
Not exhaustion,
just more fermenting,
                crystalline,
while the mind circulates around them.
Thoughts provoke
new thoughts,
    ordered, chaotic.
No grille obstructs,
    no halo.
Thought's wingèd horse rises,
    flies up
from the brain's infinity,
    throws light
in the cerebral grey,
    leaves
the physical body in a steep glide.

In the Melting Pot

I collected iron for the scrap merchant, walked
back and forth across the fields,
found rusty horseshoes in the ploughed up earth,
tobacco tins without lids,
    crumbling screws.
A little pile behind the farm
rose, every spring,
at the side of the stack
my father had prepared for pickup,
a corroded tank, a superannuated plough, worn-out tools,
a barometer
    for reading the world.
All the things had belonged to someone,
been used for something,
emptied, made useful,
                    thrown away.
The world was full of pieces,
of iron, of wood, of glass,
grown-ups had got rid of,
forgotten or replaced,
strewn about, lost.
Waste, rubbish, junk
                connected with memory,
unlike
when in a totally unfamiliar place
I am lost in thought about some unknown device.
    What was it used for?
I stand one light-filled morning
in a market in another country
with a bent hinge
unscrewed from a door or a cabinet
    remember the scrap merchant,
who drove from farm to farm,
his bulging load of discarded items.
Iron, which in liquid form
could become plates, pipes,
cylinders, gears, sculptures,
perhaps a Robert Jacobsen
    the sun would sparkle in,
objects which in a single flash
could generate new meaning. Acquire new life.

44

Between Østerport and World's End

He is wrapped in a big coat.
  I am wrapped in a big coat.
He does not move from the spot.
  I stand just as still.
He looks at the rows of cars gliding by.
  I also look at the cars gliding by.
He clears his throat.
  I do the same.
He says: – *It's cold today.*
  I say: – *Yes, it's cold today.*
He says: – *Yesterday it wasn't quite as bad.*
  I say: – *Yes, it wasn't quite as bad.*
He casts a glance at the clock,
the bus is late again today.
  I cast a glance at the clock,
the minutes grow, everyone will be late...
He sighs.
  I sigh.
He stares up into the winter sky for a long time.
  I stare up into the winter sky for a long time.
Intensified silence under the canopy
in the midst of the traffic.
A little girl comes along with a dog on a leash,
it sniffs at us both,
                jumps up –
first at him,
  then at me.
Out of the corner of my eye I look at the man at the bus stop,
a half-blind mirror placed in the city.
His face is wrinkled as a walnut.
  Perhaps soon mine will be too?

Saddle

At the museum I see a saddle
for a camel –
in the midday heat inhale
    a faint smell
recognised by generations,
                the smell of leather.
Consciousness pulls up
the tent pegs.
…And then off
between barren rocks
and thorny plants
to haul storms
and deserts through me.
Clothes stick in the heat,
insects bite.
Sun and drifting sand
    scratch the heart.
No trace is left
in the sand-dunes,
which the wind drifts.
I move on
when dawn shows up,
    follow the caravan,
the flow of everything on its way
                in waylessness.

Pass, Passport, Passaporto, Etc.

Am I as ugly as in the photo?
Can I be let through,
once I have handed the official
my passport with its old visas
and its rain of stamps?
Am I really a wanted terrorist?
The man at the desk gauges the open passport,
belonging to the European Union,
    issued
by the chief of police in Copenhagen.
The man looks up at me, checks his computer,
for perhaps I am on the run
                    – perhaps not?
Possibly just
    plain suspicious?
I wait. The queue grows behind me,
while my data is scrutinised.
I am not a criminal, not
a trafficked woman
nor an illegal immigrant
have no forged identity papers
have not smuggled cigarettes or stuffed
other unlawful things into my luggage.
I have no previous convictions
there is nothing to go on, but perhaps
that is a mystery?
    The body is not national,
it passes easily into dreams
mountain ranges, rivers and oceans,
    routes traced by swallows.
I want
    the clouds' passport
valid for travel to all countries and back.

The Philosophy of the Gate

The gate is open –
a parenthesis, a threshold,
   a starting-point,
an entrance to the world
or an exit.
Will life
have a chance
or death
   an opportunity?
Something is put behind, perhaps
the gate will slam shut
   forever.
Something else waits ahead,
whether it is paradise
or hell
no one knows. Only
that the unforeseen
       comes to meet us
as white music or black.

Moving Day

I wake from a dream
    my mother has had,
just as she wakes with a start
    from my nightmare.
Our waters have parted –
yet we reach one another
                    bubblingly clear:
I sit in the sun, nineteen years old,
between bed, table, chair and what
I actually own,
my clothes and my beloved books,
packed into boxes, crammed
into the trailer.
My father starts the tractor, the sound
is familiar, but the day
    vibrates tensely.
The trailer with its load
sways and rocks forwards across the courtyard,
small stones reflect the light, crunch
and grate as the wheels
roll over them.
    Light, water,
    a floating axis...
I wave from the trailer to my mother.
She takes root
            in her tears.
But why cry
on a festive day like this?
My mother collects herself, waves back
loves me enough
            to let go.
Our waters part –
I'm a salmon
on my way up the stairs
in a silvery   leap   after leap.

Sinking to the Bottom in Our Own Heaven

Filling the ears with sound
of cicadas, the lungs
with increasing warmth.
The radiance of caresses
a black
and southern night,
where the scent of the pines
spreads out and we
are more alive
than in all the day.
Singing wings cut
through the air,
rivers burn,
    avalanches
of constellations
dazzle
inner cranial walls.

Lost and Found

Lost and Found it says promisingly – but I've
got nothing back.
A cloakroomful and more will be available
should anyone think
    of following in my footsteps.
A handbag with both keys and purse
left behind in my pure girlhood,
between hard-hitting drinks
at a nightclub in London.
My grandfather sent money,
                    – So that it doesn't happen again! –
More insight has come to me
with each journey,
but the list of forgotten or lost objects
    is a ceaselessly sighing river:
A midnight-coloured velvet jacket on a plane
from Ljubljana to Zurich, from where
at a height of only 20,000 feet
I saw Alps in the sun, black and white.
My best silver ring with an oval onyx stone
bought in Bergen with my first foreign fee.
A sweater acquired in Madrid and gone missing
a few hours later in the train to Barcelona.
A pair of ear-muffs made in China,
bought in Copenhagen, lost one foggy winter night in Milan.
Sandals from Cuba in a labyrinthine Istanbul,
a scarf in the crowds of a department store in Moscow,
sunglasses at a gas station outside Charleston,
a lightweight umbrella at a café table in Geneva
when the sun finally broke through rain clouds,
a nightdress in bed in Toronto,
when a fire alarm cut through MY sleep,
a folding knife with scissors, nail cleaner
and corkscrew near an Icelandic waterfall,
a bright red belt in a ruined wardrobe
in Granada, Nicaragua,
a water bottle in Jerusalem,
an earring on the back seat of a taxi in New York,
a wristwatch among sand and seashells

51

on a Greek island
        and thus my sense of time,
my sleep on a barge in the Nile
            and consequently my sense of logic,
but worse,
    my heart in Paris.

Mysterious Bridge

With my lipstick
a poet from Cyprus is reading
her poems in Turkish.
A woman asking
to borrow my lipstick
is for a second
more overarching of borders
than driving from one country
    to another.
My lipstick now speaks
on her lips.
Suddenly I'm one kiss closer to
    her language.
With my lipstick
she is reading
a poem about a man
who is like a pendulum. He
sways   incessantly
between two women.
That could have been
    my life
my lipstick was reading poems about.
An arrow
would have kissed
the nape of his neck.

The Dream of the East

The historic centre in a Chinese city
is levelled by heavy cranes.
Village-like neighbourhoods
are cleared away for skyscrapers.
Futuristic glass, concrete and steel
    replace wood.
Rice paper lanterns
              that swayed red in the breeze
are superseded by a hospital-like glare.
Small, winding shopping streets straightened
to make room for offices,
for supermarkets, for bulging department stores.
Video commercials or bent neon
    flicker from the facades of buildings.
The swarm of cyclists and pedestrians
    gives way to cars whizzing past.
Young women have put on
the smallest miniskirts,
originals or copies
from European fashion houses.
Young men are dressed as at home,
as they hang out on the squares
with skateboards
    and cans of Coca-Cola.
I wanted to capture a glimpse of the East
before it mirrored the West –
but shops that once
sold goods made of bamboo
offer nothing more than plastic,
and the little drugstore on the corner
with thousands of drawers
of dried seahorses, snakeskins,
powder from rhinoceros and tiger bones,
    a zoo
    preserved in boxes and jars,
has now been replaced by a 7-Eleven.
I have listened to the poetry here
    which has long listened to ours.
Perhaps I don't sense the changes

in my own country, when I stare
myself blind at them nearsightedly.

The dragon with the forked tongue
spells at once to East and West.

Oasis

The journey is good
because it stops again,
the journey is to and from,
    there and back.
If it doesn't stop
it is something else,
    escape, exile, banishment,
steps that lead to nothing.
The mere thought
of its ending
    is a pure oasis
where sand is washed away
from hands and eyes,
and the bottle filled
    with water from the source.

Landing

My body has landed,
it has set a full stop to the journey.
And the nervous system,
which had adapted
to other latitudes,
is accustoming itself to the familiar again.
My body has landed,
the luggage is there,
                    but the soul
is apparently doing fine in New Delhi
among birds and reflected light,
    it has not returned.
It sees dogs playing in the dust, sees
women in colourful saris and sandals
walk swaying
with pyramids of fruit
in baskets on their heads.
It listens to young women chirping
like birds in a bush, it listens
and understands immediately
    without comprehending the words.
My body has arrived
at its own home,
has lugged the suitcase up the stairs
and unlocked the front door.
It had no problem
finding its way back
to the cold moonlit nights,
                    but the soul
still sits under a tree watching
a little girl fan away the flies,
while she plays with her chair in the grass
in a park
where it's warm and quiet
    and the sun is low.
I return
with wide-awake eyes to see
my own world again,
    soon the soul will be here, too.

Through September

I walk through the autumn landscape
of stubble, red rowanberries
and blackberry bushes,
    breathe the smells
of long ago.
It is my mother's month,
her light,
        always her September.
The sun is mild, my father
comes in to see her
from the field.
Under high, night-clear stars, too,
my mother will be there
                    in September.
Elderberries ripen,
cherry plums fall to the earth,
the roses are fragrant.
Apples, figs, pears
are picked.
The ripest fig on the tree
that grows along the white south wall
in the courtyard,
        my mother eats.
The war is far away,
almost forgotten in the sun,
but my father cannot
harrow down
        the sorrow of her youth.
It is an earth-darkness
that throws itself even into
the year's most golden-yellow light,
where the world, when I look at it,
                        lifts its gaze.

Tomorrow Does Not Come Back

Horses in a field
stand flicking their tails,
they are
what they are:
horses in a field.
          And hope
of change
in that pouring rain of hopelessness
that burns right now.

Nomad

I live only a stone's throw
from Africa.
A click on the computer
    and I soar
from Denmark to Cape Town,
to Kabul, Tehran or
Rio de Janeiro without
                putting down roots.
Has it become easier
to choose one's life, or have I
already been swallowed
                by options?
A click
and I land
in Damascus, Dubai
or on a steppe in Kazakhstan.
A new country
is not identical to
long exile,
    I can quickly return.
For the nomads of today
it doesn't matter
if here
is *here* or *there*,
they don't need
to saddle up an animal and pitch a tent.
Here is here
    everywhere,
a very solitary pleasure.

The Gremlin Stays the Same

There is a condition that cannot
be left behind –
it is everywhere,
      the quivering unrest
that ignites the mind's lighter fluid.
If I wake up at home
   it is in my bed,
if I wake up abroad
   it is also in my bed,
the enemy
   that faithfully loves me.
The quivering unrest finds its way, no matter
where I am.
I only wish
it would stay away
but it knows the route
   even in the dark
or on very lonely days
   with a large amount of people.
It finds its way like sparks
   in leaps
to trigger the explosion
               that crushes rocks to sand.

The Friend Who Is a Stranger

To the stranger
　who scarcely remembers who I am
I confide details
that would cause major conflicts
if anyone at home were let in on them.
Among the skeletons of migrating birds
even double Gordian knots
can be untied.
It's the Irishwoman
resident in South Africa, who in Montreal
navigates like a chaos pilot in squalls,
　shortly before I crash.
She sees
　what is invisible to the eye.
She sweeps
　the clouds away.
She recovers
　a sunken treasure.
The shadow
I will not let go,
　　　　　it is my future.
I will probably never meet her again
　and if I do,
Patricia is so close a friend
that she will no longer
give me advice, but have
　　　　　my warmest thanks.

Wanted

– Mind your step,
says a voice over the loudspeakers
above the airport's moving walkways.
– Mind your step,
DNA from an emptied wallet
thrown away at the harbour in Malmö
matches the DNA
from a holiday home burglary
near Hornbæk Plantation
matching a series of break-ins
committed in broad daylight at villas
in Copenhagen's northern suburbs,
matching the DNA from a street
robbery in Kolding,
matching the DNA
from a bestial rape
in the centre of Hamburg, matching
the DNA from someone murdered
in the heart of Amsterdam's
Red Light District.
– Mind your step,
the trail does not lie,
                    the escape
belongs to the wanted man
again and again
            the same –
only the profile remains.

Centre

The low sun over zinc-grey roofs in Paris,
the gentle gleam in March, an evening bird
sings.
This gleam, these minutes
before the light disappears
   so precious
after a Nordic winter.
Behind closed eyes the colour
                  morning red
like the sound of the doorbell
that at this moment is ringing
   homely
in an alien world.
The visit of a familiar
voice,
   breathing of snow-flowers.
Where else should I be, if not here?

The Neighbour in the Yellow House

A door is opened to the neighbour
in the yellow house.
I live on one side of the street,
he lives on the other,
    but the street does not unite us.
The sun is shining, the wall of his house
is illuminated.
Birds in the air
cast shadow on the wall
before they disappear
    like needlescript across the sky.
The double door is wide open
to an apartment above the one
    I am temporarily living in.
My thoughts float
across the street to the balcony
with climbing springtime greenness
and an overturned chair, into the room
laden with residues
of labyrinthine dreams and conversations.
What separates us
                is an open door.
The darkness escapes, and the light
is let in to the neighbour,
    who doesn't find me either,
and whom I will not get to know
because I am on a journey
    onward,
but whose dwelling
I cannot resist
    allowing my eyes to move into,
as I darken on the way
                from myself to myself.

65

Compass

In the embrace I see
a bird pass –
its wings, its movement
                    onward.
See tomorrow fly away,
but first land here
    in a magnetic now.
The compass needle quivers,
the days
arrow after arrow on their way.
My footprints
    in many countries,
but far more in the ash of dreams.

The Words Travel

I live in another country, but even so
don't leave my home.
The alphabet I take with me
and the structures of the grammar,
the words' meanings and emphases.
    No matter where on the globe
I settle,
I live in the language
    I was born into.
No storm of other languages
capsizes mine.
I am *I*
      in my own language –
dreaming in what accidentally
became my mother tongue.
I write at home,
        write abroad,
everywhere the same:
The words have hearts of migrating birds,
dissection shows,
    they want to *reach* someone,
    and I live with these
bird-words, their singing and hoarse cries.

Farewell

– *See you*, we say
with a smile after a meeting,
where embers shot sparks
up into the darkness, and we forgot
the pain
as if a future
   existed,
a glow of imminent
        reunion.

Detour

Wild geese are gathering on the field
soon the whole flock will rise,
flying up over the woods, out across the water.
An ocean rolls inside me
   wide open.
I am too slow
for quick changes,
        too quick
for things to go so slowly that life
                 becomes futureless.
Dreams start
   even before one learns to walk.
From the other side of the Atlantic
I see better
what Scandinavia is –
the black duckling, the white swan,
Ibsen, Strindberg, Kierkegaard,
   gravity, melancholy, irony,
the wind settling round the trees,
   no other embrace,
grey-white light of winter days,
loneliness enough
       for all.
In a street in China
where I try
to distil meaning out
of the words' acoustics
I understand my dependence
on the Danish language
         the aorta
that runs underground in my body
no matter how aimlessly I
travel around, buoyed up
by the light.
I move onward,
   the same sky seen
from different angles,
   the same Earth,
the blood's cadence sets the pace.
Each detour I make
goes through myself alone.

69

Everywhere the Wind

The wind is like a refugee without a name,
without a homeland, without an atlas
　　passes borders
towards distant horizons
crosses time zones,
does not receive a residence permit
in any country,
　　　　but sleepless rages on.
Hurries without a backpack down from the mountains,
surprises cities, fields,
whirls up earth on the move or whips
water into waves, waves into spray, dashes
through forests, past village houses, round
corners, makes the horses' manes
fly,
cuts like an axe
into my life,
　　　splitting it
　　　　　　into fear and fascination.
The wind leaves its grooved track
in the sand, in the snow, in the dust,
as if a mighty ocean
had retreated.
The wind takes voices with it,
　　　　　　　　cries of children
that make hairs rise on one's arm,
leaves tremble on the trees,
grassblades
cower.
The wind guards wildernesses,
carries birds or fire
across vast steppes.
The wind spins my life, weaves
patterns of strength and powerlessness,
　　tears
in an embrace from all directions.
It licks dry my throat and neck, continues
　　never forgotten
out across its endless territory,
　　before at last it settles
　　　　　　in the sand, in the snow, in the blood –

70

Bird with Root

Look up into the tree
and hear
a bird gather
chaos
into seven notes.

A Point Meets the Infinite

Travel away from the familiar starry sky
to nights
   with new constellations.
Travel away from landscapes remembered
down to the narrowest path in the grass
to a terrain that does not contain
my memories... It wasn't here
I skidded on my bike, not here
I plundered a cherry tree
   one black-red night.
Travel away from streets with no one in sight
in spite of the crowds,
   travel away from my adult life's part of town,
the vacuum cleaner shop, the laundry,
the kiosk, the bookshop and the fishmonger,
the roaming cats
I reflect myself in,
   free and bedraggled with sun in their fur.
Travel away from my deaf sleepwalker's route,
which looks no different
   each time I walk it,
to far away cities that have to be trudged through
all over again –
step by step, until life
                  expands,
and the self acquires its weight.
Where can I buy a loaf of bread?
   Where can I find a post office?
      Where can I sleep?
Until the meaning of memories
one sudden morning
   is broken and reassembled.
Have left what is mine,
                  but is not owned by me
until I return to the ordinariness
that's yet not
         entirely ordinary.
A swarm of eyes
   sees me.
I greet myself more awake than before:
                        Good morning.

Homecoming

When I come home from the journey
with worn soles and dusty jacket
a month has passed.
The staircase is painted in different colours
new neighbours have moved in
both above and below me.
Phone numbers have changed,
my children have left home,
the one I love
   has found someone else.
I return
with exotic gifts
   but for whom?
I arrive full of adventures,
now worthless
   to anyone.
The thirty-one white nights
of a flowering July
have been lost,
because it is winter
where I come from…
After long refusing
to recognise me,
my old cat extends
a sour welcome.
– *Take me with you next time*
so we're not apart from each other
my lips whisper in the empty space,
where a forgotten mirror shows
that my black hair has turned grey.
– *Stay at home instead*,
I hear everyone say
in the living-room full of tomorrow.

Global Sweep Day

I sweep in front of the door, shake the doormat
free of gravel and dirt, wash the doorstep
out to the stairs, vacuum
the gravel and fluff
                  from the hall's blue carpet.
And at Kro Bay in Sierra Leone
a woman is sweeping
at least as conscientiously
in front of the door of her shack
    with just one room and six small children.
The river, a drifting rubbish dump, sewer
for animals and people,
flows alongside the shack,
but in front of it
                  things must be clean.
And outside a bombed apartment in Gaza
a woman seizes a broom
and sweeps.
Walls are blown away, everything
around her is in ruins.
In the building the concrete stairs are cracked,
a spider web
of cables and wires sticks out
    from a lacerated wall.
There is no door to close
to her apartment,
        but the sweeping must be done.
There is hardly a place
that will be skipped,
not one corner of the world
                  is without pride.

Bird Table

My mother's mother put out bread
in cold weather
for the birds on the terrace. Received song
and fighting and company
in exchange.
    My mother did the same.
Put bread scraps
on a bird table
built like an open house
in front of the kitchen window,
where she could follow
every wing-beat.
    One day I will also
feed birds.
    Watch them come
to my table, where no one
will be an uninvited guest.
The smallest breadcrumbs
will summon birds
from the remotest regions,
make them flutter
above this magnetic field
    like one long summer.

Spatial Meditation

The wind's flight over the hills,
over the brushwood and the heather's arabesque,
birds perch on branches
at the top of the Norway spruce.
                              The frame shatters...
Distended nostrils intercept
a landscape. Smells
of soil and plants
tear raw after mist and rain.
Houses built
          and laid in ruins.
War, famine, raids –
blood-wet deeds,
     sometimes miracles, too.
Swords, battle-axes and coins
speak in glints from the soil's depth
     into a severed now,
gallows hills, holy springs, burial mounds.
The sun breaks through,
the air is filled with butterflies
                         and wandering souls.
The blood's flicker through the lungs and heart
multiplies
the resonance of voices.
Tracks are buried, but there are new ones,
feet on their way along the same route.
Leap-patterns of hares
          further out
                    across the sandy soil.

In Every Language

Moss climbs green, writes itself
   with free expression
out across great rocks –
the Ice Age's erratic boulders stopped
   right here.
Stacks of pine needles pile up
into a soundproof blanket,
warmly fragrant.
The clocks have no time, the hands
   flown away.
The stillness can be seen
in among the spruce trees,
   dictionaries sleep.
The silence can be heard
              in every language.

Afterwards

What is left after the journey,
after inspection
of blisters and insect bites, and before
    images retouch themselves?
Not the tiredness in one's feet
when at the end of the day the map
is folded up.
Not roads to which the lost
have given names.
Not weathered monuments
or streets where houses
threw sharp shadows.
Not museums updated to the day before yesterday,
bus trips on travel-sick winding roads
through small villages,
where black-clad widows move
on stone steps of steep stairs
or light wax candles
in whitewashed churches.
Not distances
along monotonous roads
dragged through the rain
by red rear lights.
Not the view from the mountaintop
to other mountains
in the blue.
Not the taxis, neither the legal
nor the illegal ones,
in regular service at night
between towers
embraced by darkness.
Not Sunday-quiet parks
with mirror-black lakes
or the glowing colours and the smells
of the tightly-packed market stalls,
where thanks and curses
intersect one another,
                but the cup of coffee we had together
at a random café

with the first smile of the day
                    in our eyes,
while the traffic swirled around us,
making the dust rise
   in a cloud of forgetting,
and pigeons hurriedly fly into exile.

Curiosity Cabinet

One cupboard door in the house
must be opened with especial caution,
                              for out tumble
objects bought or received
   for eternal remembrance.
From an Italian flea market
an Aladdin-like oil lamp,
which in many years of my youth
   repeatedly brought luck.
As did
different-coloured Egyptian scarab beetles
and a magic male figure
from New Zealand.
A pair of reindeer antlers from Norway, my first trophy,
since wheedled away –
a dagger in a leather sheath from the same place, a pen
from Germany, dried olive leaves
from Israel, a shirt of finest silk,
from Vietnam, a ceramic dish
from Greece, a bracelet of silver
from Turkey, a bag
from Vienna, a gold key
with a religious motif
awarded in Colombia with the hope
   that one day I would get on the right track,
fringed black shawl from Portugal, plaited horsehair
and a mask from Mexico, music
from Argentina, so the dancing can continue,
a bowl from a temple in Japan, marble sculptures
from Carrara, hand-cut glass
from Romania, a box
of seashells and a giant conch
from Cuba as a fee
for a reading, a primordial rock
from Uluru, Australia's navel,
a kurta from India, a candle
from Paris, a leopard-patterned jumpsuit
from the Twin Towers,
   which, before anyone had any suspicions,
already cast the shadow of destruction

80

over New York,
a sealskin belt from Nuuk, a foxfur
from Helsinki, a sheepskin from Tórshavn
books in languages I can't read, postcards
from all sorts of museums, a copper pot
with four miniature cups from Sarajevo, a mug
with a motif of Hässelby Castle, calligraphy
with coral red stamp from Kunming, from Cairo
a plaster cat that lost one ear
after a confrontation with a very living cat
on a windowsill in Copenhagen
on Rosenvængets Sideallé,
a melted ice sculpture
from St Petersburg, birdsong
from the Baltics, and from a proud people:
The Ukrainian Flag.
    In addition, T-shirts and carrier bags
for the rest of my days.
From my grandfather I have learned to say:
– *Thank you, that is too much,*
when something is well-intentioned, but really bad
so I am not lying,
because it IS
                far too much.
The tea from Ledbury and the coffee from Skopje
    has been drunk,
as has the cheese from Switzerland and Slovakia,
the foie gras from Budapest
and the chocolates from Brussels
    have been eaten
but otherwise I keep
these finds, or gifts.
Smells from large parts of the globe escape
when I open the cupboard door a little,
memories like raw material
for further meditation and revision,
                            or reminiscences enough
for years at a retirement home
swarm to meet me... All these countries
    exist in me,
impressions flicker by
like crash barriers on a motorway;
I have not longed for more than one life.

81

Camera

Waiting several days
for the mist to drift in
    over the island.
Sitting on the rocks
in the wind and waiting
in the Baltic's sea-smell,
until one day it's there,
    and yet the fog
won't let itself
be immortalised.
The white mist
that approaches over the grass
and slowly engulfs me,
    it's said,
is not just too pretty
to photograph –
it settles like a cloud
    in the eye
of the one who soon will die.

Rest in Motion

Find rest
in birds that drift
on black wings
in wedges cut
across the sky.
Is that why
we are buried
in the earth
lying on our backs?

The Tracks Are Made

Under my feet
the Earth vaults
in silent rotation.
　In my blood
were two sons
with the same longing
that dwells in every bird.
　In my soul
a sun's explosion.

III

With a Child On My Shoulders

Walking with a child on my shoulders
holding onto its ankles,
while it puts its hands
                on my forehead.
Resting in myself
despite the fire in the centre of the earth.
Walking with the child, so it sees
what I see
in the evening light that blood-red
screws itself into the earth.
Seeing what the child sees
talking about what meets
us both, believing
our own eyes,
    listening to each other.
Leading the child
                but letting it choose for itself.
The road is not hidden,
it must be found or find us
as the air calls
            on the birds.
Roads continue
To be roads
that open in streams
without being understood.
Foot tracks, blind tracks
                future tracks.
Walking and walking, not to approach
a goal,
but to consider what
is approaching,
    take part in the delta of dreams.
Walking and walking with an inherited
idea that
the story hardly ends   here.

SALAMANDER SUN

This now
sets the future as
focus,
gives it a face –

Joy

First is joy,
   smuggled across the border
      through a narrow tunnel.
The night is over, drowned in the sea,
   buried in the earth,
      thousands of years passed alone.
Smells that already existed,
   closely surround,
      horses snort in the stable.
Wake with light,
   see shadow-play on the wallpaper,
      hear birds in bushes and ivy.
The grown-ups' voices and laughter,
   a safe landing place
      on the other side of the wall.
First is the morning garden
   in sun,
      its illumination of the heart.
Apples fall in the warm grass,
   insects rise
      up from flowers' petal depth.
First is openness,
   that soon closes,
      faceless.
First is trust,
   that is easily swallowed
      by galactic fear.
First is joy,
   that newborn flows
      towards the world, dreams it.
Then follows sorrow, then follows anger,
   then someone says:
   – *Peace be with it.*
Life is death that is coming,
   but first is joy.

Discovery

Hours in pram. Alone. See spoon on road. Grab.
Push away. Spoon again. Fly. Hit. Teeth. Tongue.
Spoon scrapes across mouth. Spit out cod-liver oil. Pinch
lips together. Walk across the yard. Crunch, crunch on the gravel. Fall.
Crawl. Gather stones. Rummage about. Eat earth and gravel.
Spit out. Scream. Be brushed down. Be picked up. Sit high
on father's arm. Touch stubble. Smell father. Pull hair.
Tug towards. Get kiss. See animals. Bull. Cow. Moo... Breathe
smells in the stables. The voices of the grooms. Pail. Gently stroke
the horse's muzzle. Again. Again. Hours in pram. Alone.
In harness. Rock. Sway so the whole pram sways. Chained fire.
Fling rattle. Suck fingers. Sucking. Shadows on the wall.
Jump. Birds between leaves. Cheep... In the afternoon
orange juice. Pieces of apple. Cram in mouth. Chew.
Drool. Turn buttons. Find things on floor. Peel.
Suck. Taste. Roll the ball. To. Fro. On the carpet.
Bite her leg. Because she wants to go out of the room,
the nanny. Not alone again. Pull at the doll. Swing.
Slap. Let go. Fish up a brick. Put in mouth.
Sit down. In the playpen. Hammer brick hard
on bars. Throw brick. Up again. The dog's
nose. Bow-wow... Poke finger into its nose.
Wet. Touch its puppies. Pat. Slap. Plunge
hands into its coat. Be lifted. Bathed. Egg yolks
in hair, mother washes. Water in eyes. Eat porridge. Full.
Eat up. Spoon scrapes across mouth. Crawl up
the stairway's many stairs. Mother's light slaps from behind. Away,
away, as swift ye may. Upstairs to sleep. Be put aside.
Up to the first floor. Alone. Door ajar. Good night. Rain
dots the window. Other sounds in the room. Dry creaking.
Strange sounds. Dark sounds. Too awake to sleep.

91

Stillborn Brother

Splinters in my mouth, when I bite
the glass of squash
one lonely afternoon on the stone steps.
    Tears.
My mother's, too, because
    my brother
didn't breathe
when he was born.
The grapes in the greenhouse, mist-blue clusters
in the heat under the glass
with the sky and the clouds.
    The silence.
    The lack of words.
The sparrows don't sing down in the garden
in the bushes under the trees –
they mourn from the branches
    amidst soft rustling in the leaves.
My mother picks splinters out
of my bloody mouth, summer,
rocks my burning thoughts
    to rest.
Her eyes reflect
the boy she has given birth to
but not seen
    the brother
I didn't get. Not this time.
White flowers float out
into the dark,
    their scent of madness.
Another time... Perhaps a sister.
Sleep-river, moon-eyes,
                    pulse, light,
seven-league shadows.
I dream about my dead brother
    day and night I dream,
                    look always
for *him*, whom only my father has seen.

Lifeline

The mouth climbs through the hair, whispers words
   against my ear,
the last thing I sense before I sleep,
the first thing I hear when I wake.
The words lead out of
the borderlands of fevered darkness
weave themselves into a line
to grasp hold of,
                a leap into the day.
From the lips a line to the housemaids. They repeat
the names of the days, the months, the numbers,
   in the grass beneath the chestnut trees.
A line to the grooms. They tell stories
that smell of mould and sweat,
   of animal skin in the darkness of the stables.
To the boys, who play at war, wound, flame-red blood,
unfamiliar words for what I know,
   and words for what no one has talked about before.
To my mother in the serving pantry,
bent over flowers and scissors.
Songs, speech, litanies of abyss
   fly above the busyness of her fingers.
To my father's bedtime stories night after night,
the books he reads to me,
stairs leading up to new halls at midnight
                   in a light-filled castle.
The names of things, gradually more recollection,
names of animals and people,
   someone says you and *Pia*,
says *Monica*, my sister's name.
The name my dead brother would have had,
   no one says.
Voices open door after door in the castle
into what has not been given a name,
               and waits to receive one –
into the newly invented, the radiant.
Words for light and darkness,
words transparent and mysterious,
         before *I* becomes *I*.

Ode to Freud

The groom and the maid in front of me on the bed,
in her chamber the man from the stables, I
at the foot. Play ship. They have the pillows,
straight upright I sit. The groom coaxes
the maid away from me, she rebuffs him.
With me. She is going to read stories,
she has promised. *Snow White*, she has promised,
but he squeezes in, blocking her view
so she can't see me... so she
forgets I ought to be asleep... His
arms around her, his body against
hers, squeezes, unbuttons, their legs
they weave together, she utters
sounds I did not know could come
from a human being. Only from the animals
in the stables. He thinks I don't see,
though I see. His socks, wet hay
I breathe in. The maid's breast. The groom's
hand. I see. The groom changes colour,
to red and purple he changes. His
kiss, where she is white. I see. Flick.
Like a stick on bird's eggs fallen out
of the nest, down on the wet earth.
My mother and father have gone in the car. To
Copenhagen they have gone and haven't
that smell of the turnips in the clamp that flows
from the groom and the maid... The groom
no longer sees me here at the mast,
he doesn't see anyone but the maid. I
see myself. See that I'm watching,
sunk into myself. Forget
again that I see. In front of me. The two of them
pell-mell in a heap...
Vanish into their sounds. Into their
warm smells, the groom's and the maid's...
The ship breaks free of its moorings,
glides from the shore with me on board. Out
on a splashing sea I am taken,
keel over, don't drown. See and see. Sail.

94

Banishment

Early summer, the smell of new mown grass, sun-stillness in the garden
– but in anger
I tear
   the heads
from a large cluster of flowers,
the yellow, yellow ones in the flower bed, those
no one else must have, the ones
I can no longer reach out my hand for.
Only clothes and toys, my mother and father,
sister and grey cat, the one I found in the barn,
                              go with me.
The mirror doesn't see itself. Deadly
leap from the straw stack with the boys.
No angel intervenes,
   wipes sweat from my brow.
The tree with the red apples, the birds, the brook
along the garden, the animals' throat-warmth, their breath.
   Shears. Knife. Scythe. Gone, gone.
Goodbye, grooms and maids,
                  goodbye, everyone I've played with.
Those familiar rooms I can't
lean against, behind whose doors no one will
sit and wait any more. I have
no choice, can only leave the place
on earth that was *ours*, was *mine*,
where the world approached me.
Even before I've gone
                I am longing to be back.
As if time can go on outside the farm
   on Lake Esrum,
as if the stars can shine somewhere else,
                 the words find a mouth.

95

No Man's Land

My grey cat vanishes,
or has it acquired a new life
    at Nivå Brickworks?
At night I hear it calling...
Search for it, search again the next day.
Live in a vacuum, while my father
looks for another farm,
but learn in sun and dust to cycle,
shoot myself forward like a mainspring,
    ever further out
on Vibevej, along the residential gardens.
Lilacs, laburnums,
an olfactory orgy to sweep past.
Shall I vanish like the cat,
for there is no one to play with,
    and over the summer
I lose
    tooth after tooth in my hollowed hand.
When my mother takes an afternoon nap
with no hands on the clock
the first one falls out,
    white,
but leaving
    a bloody hole
the tongue's tip wants to drill down into
– instead of calling, speaking.
Taste of iron in the mouth. Blood words.
Cave language. Tongue pit.
A tooth
    white
as a daisy growing in the grass
in the garden of the house we rent
    and under whose roof my mother in the rain
now and then sings
                'Solitude Road'.
In the house with creaky stairs
and smells of strangers
    there is a studio
we may not enter, my sister and I,
    there I seek refuge –

96

sit for hours on the floor, contemplate
the radiant pictures'
            vanishing grey.

Godmother

The lowest part of my body
there is long no name for
and is not familiar
like the face, arms or legs.
The lowest part of my body belongs to
   the time of fables or myths,
it's a giddy and joyous labyrinth,
only visible
     in the experimental mirror
my godmother
gives me one day.
Her
I will live with if a plane
                 crashes
with my mother and father,
or the house burns down while I'm at school.
Since then I've
   believed
in godmothers, mirror mysteries and naked delusions.

Prepositions

An eraser is put *in front of* the box, *behind* the box, *on* the box,
   under the box.
We push one another aside, boys and girls,
to see the teacher put the eraser
towards, away *from* or back *to* the box,
   near the box, *in* the box, *between*
this box for erasers and another for pencils.
Or more erasers lie scattered
   around the box.
The origin of the universe was not an explosion *in* space,
but *of* space,
not an explosion *in* time,
but *of* time,
   whereby both space and time were born...
Order is brought into a breathless swarm, time and space
are put in place by means of prepositions,
which not only indicate one's relation to things,
but also dream about them
               far away *from* or close *to*.
If the soul
is located *inside* – or elsewhere,
   is not known with certainty,
but the brain sees a lot with language's smallest words,
   that look out of nothing,
sandwiched between others they show
   where one is.
The lesson is over; so it's *out* to the steel-hard beat of the playground,
then *into* the classroom again and down *on* the chair.
I don't reach resting pulse,
I am ignited waiting in every cell,
   ready to move.
Changing positions are revealed,
               being *in* the middle of or on the way *to*.

Game of Dice

On the table a triangle of cardboard folded upwards
like a snow-clad mountain, blue-white
like the milk in the bottles
with tops of aluminium foil.
The mountain must be climbed at the rate
   only rolls of the dice determine.
A roll, the dice as it falls –
and worst: to end up
with the abominable snowman
close to the mountain's summit.
Snow-slides and avalanches force
   the players to wait.
A roll, the dice as it falls, its rolling
across the table, abrupt halt –
its star-shaped eyes: misadventure
sweeps the players back to the nearest hut,
   even home
to the foot of the mountain.
I try to avoid every danger,
defeat CHANCE
by practising hitting sixes.
Even change the dice
in the hope it will make a difference,
but read again and again
unexpected constellations.
I gather all my energy
   gather myself to a single point.
CHANCE won't let itself be abolished,
it shows its number, the eyes light up:
fear most of all being caught,
not escaping the snowman's grip.
Throw by throw I approach
the summit along the winding path,
set off above the snowline into
   the unpredictable.
The other players' deafening silence
   if I win,
their deep, throaty hooting and cheering,
   if I lose.

Inside Edge

The lake with the drowned kittens,
   on it
we fly on skates, cut
   into glassy winter.
Outside edge and inside edge
performed by my mother,
with a new baby in her belly,
   backward glide
with bottom pushed back
and arms out horizontally,
the skates sliding
   from side to side –
but especially
the grinding sound
of newly sharpened metal
   against ice,
a whish of snow-sparks
leaps in the light.
The lake with the drowned kittens,
   on it
we fly on skates,
when the ice is thick enough
                to forget
paws that flailed in the air,
claws that stretched out,
the blindly sinking creatures
that floundered in the sack
              with the heavy stone.
The bubbles that for long
   floated
on the black water
where the rings had a centre
   like shooting targets
on maps that showed the range
of the missiles on Cuba.

Autumn Day

My father at the writing table, I near the window,
from where chilly air blows in.
Crisp rustling scrapes
through the silence of the living room
when he turns a page of the newspaper.
From moment to moment
I stand and watch the leaves
    that rise
in an unforeseen dance in the wind,
                            a fiery rain of colours,
are carried onward high above the lawn,
    out to the day's most extreme periphery.
I don't look across at my father,
only notice we are in the room together,
    that *we* are, that *the world* is,
        that something *beyond* is.
The trees let go of the dead leaves,
they drop down into the garden,
    are caught up, hurled away
in an unceasing motion.
My father reads at the writing table,
    and I
am born in the whirling.
I swallow the world in a single glance,
    or it swallows me.
I am there
       and am not there.
Like that I'm most present, free-
floating, wide awake,
as now, when I still bear the sight with me,
    without the burning glass of consciousness
    igniting the dry foliage,
just see the leaves carried onward. Myself carried onward.

Pupa

Around me a pupa's white web
of silence.
Winter sleep has robbed my familiar body
   and in exchange
given new dreams' shadow-speech.
Safest: to ensure
   safety.
Behind the house's whitewashed walls I lock the door
when I take a bath, stuff cotton wool
   in the keyhole.
Time does not stand still.
My naked body has begun to resemble
the picture of a body
I happened to see in a sticky booklet in the woods.
The nose doesn't go with the eyes,
the eyes don't go with the mouth, the teeth are too big
   if I smile.
Arms and legs have no sense of direction,
   don't balance with the body.
It constantly changes clothes, turns
away from inquisitive gazes
that move me further in
   to uncertainty.
On photos paint my face out
   with black ink.
That body I see
   is differently the same.
That face I see
   isn't mine –
I don't yet know
         what is me.
I laugh too loud or suddenly sob
   without knowing why I'm crying.
I am neither nor, I am endless waiting
   in secret.
Stare one summer's day
into the house's tumultuous mirrors,
   as if a truth
finally blazing might reveal itself there.

103

The Grass Stands Up

Outside the brain, a snowstorm of chestnut blossom
bicycles with schoolbags thrown on the verge
   and us
at the end of the avenue near the main road
where *away* begins,
         and an eye
watches from up in the house perhaps.
The flowers sail mutely through the air,
   a zone between yes and no –
a boundary erased by panic daylight.
A trap is set up, I am lured in,
the lid snaps shut, the cage
                captures us both.
The blood rushes in foggy rings,
clouds drown between the chestnut trees
in waves of grass,
        the earth's interior is burning.
There I descend, as something calls,
renounces everything along the way.
The wrong boy and the right girl
or the right boy and the wrong girl,
spelt by birdsong
     in the treetops.
Not like on film, not like in books.
   The grass stands up again.
Afterwards it can only be miraculously
better, even though the first kiss
   sprouts into the next ones,
so that beauty can be obtained
   from its shadow,
when someone puts a hand on my heart.

Partisan

Music on a foreign preserve, rhythms that thud
up through floors, out through walls.
The heat of the dancing in whirls, flying
lizards on a dusty floor
to which a new moon
                    lends its light.
Conversations with unbuttoned blouse
through the night in a house with doors
that open, one by one,
exits to new entrances.
                    Come...
It starts with a gleam
rising in the brain,
with the seed in the womb
                    a wild wind of forces –
a sudden morning clarity,
the urge to start a protest march
    against anyone who hinders a meeting.
The compass's needle shows *here*,
shows *now*:
        The dream of the real.
The priest smothers my faith with dogma,
mercilessly fights
    my lovesickness,
as the buds of the beech burst,
                    and the sun races down,
strikes the green leaves, strikes us on the forest floor,
    shines over everything.
At the priest's I opt out
    shortly after my confirmation,
wave farewell to the church, which has no room for
double-lit joy,
        doesn't understand a fourteen-year-old.

Future Plan

My father gives me a spiral bound notebook
for précis of the books I read one after the other.
At Christmas I open a transparent box
with pens in twelve colours, immediately begin
to make notes with the pink one
on Charlotte Brontë's *Jane Eyre*,
a few days later write in blue
about John Steinbeck's *The Wayward Bus*,
then in red
about Alan Sillitoe's *Saturday Night and Sunday Morning*.
If I become a librarian,
    (as my parents suggest)
there will be time for husband and children.
No one imagines
        I will write books,
but in the school's jotters with yellow covers
meant for essays entered in ink
    I am writing my first poems.
As a librarian I will have all the books
    I could want,
will not have to think about due-back dates,
    (they remind me).
In the evening I can belong to the family, sit
by the fire in the house, feel the warmth on my face,
    let my eyes respond to sparks in leaps.
As a stone rolls out of its shadow,
the soul, acrobatic, wants to
escape the Sunday depressions
behind the closed doors and windows,
    I sense.
It wants to sail on open oceans, on rivers
like rivers of fire between green slopes,
see mountains, desert landscapes, snow-covered earth,
find its way into the narrow streets of big cities with odours
of urine, sweat and incense,
    of which I've heard tell,
it wants to be charged with the energy of the alien.
If I listen to my parents' advice,
each day I will think of Borges,
    hope

each morning to be found
                      by a magic sunrise,
go from dark matter across the threshold of pain
to secret, labyrinthine worlds,
   be woken by a dream there.

Freedom in France

There is talk of freedom in France
of occupation of universities,
of students in the streets,
                        it is heard as an echo
in North Zealand, it spreads
to a house in Hellebæk.
In May's flying green colours
  we meet
night after night in a room under the attic,
move into a hope for a world
                        open to all.
Martin Luther King has been killed,
but the vision lives with the combined forces
  of a flock of birds.
Fights in the streets of Paris
                        call us together.
We discuss freedom
  and the expectation of it rises higher.
We talk about freedom,
                so it exists
as a counter to the status quo.
Even for someone who is only 5 feet 3 inches tall
and weighs 109 pounds there is the prelude
                        to freedom.
We feel it
like the solar wind from space,
a floating sensation in the body,
that acquires form
                when it sets itself
and other bodies in motion
                starts a rebellion.
There is talk of freedom,
  at least we have the key,
when we pull the pin of thought grenades,
break a state that is sealed,
                see boundaries move,
move boundaries,
        see new signs of life
in the molecules' formations between us,

108

alone united with alone

     in each other
and in yearning's light forget death
 is there,
since the idea has a grip on us –
and then suddenly hear the birds switch off.

Purple Pussycat

First, lessons in Shakespeare, Shelley and Poe,
on a school bench in July
in Bournemouth.
Infinity of new words
   transfixed
by the chalk's white noise on a blackboard, explosions
from neurite to dendrite
light up accessible paths in the brain.
Then expeditions round the back of sleep
                           into London's nightlife:
The Purple Pussycat Disco,
is open 'from eight till late'.
Here the body changes gear, here it bursts
its hard shell,
   lets itself be hurled
              into a healing dance.
The brain is left behind
   by the mind,
when the pulse beats wing-strokes,
and the world in a rush of readiness
                  comes condensed to greet it.
We have landed on an alien planet –
move across the lunar floor
between gravel and segments of dreams
   with the weightless steps of astronauts.
I glimpse the many gazes, wisdom of altered
bodies.
The world is real
           and the cratered night a now of pouring sun.

Macro-Collective Break

In a society within a society
I live. With a plaited leather
hair-band and without much clothing.
Wake up in the forenoon
with quivering eardrums
to sounds of rock that thunders
between the tents on the site,
so the birds in the terrain
must abandon their marking.
As if on starry nights
I seesaw and sway and fall
asleep to the swell
of high-frequency concerts.
I use the makeshift
shower. Buy from the
temporary grocer's. Eat
a planned hotchpotch
of biodynamic vegetables
and unpolished rice. Of sour
and sweet balancing
with bitter and salt. Spend
a few sober hours in the middle of the day
at spontaneous happenings
in the sand. Or listen to
discussions at communal meetings.
About anarchy. About utopia. Life
outside the existing laws
turns out to be subject to other
laws. I lie in the grass and laugh
in an afterdaze at the sun. An
endless laughter. Or attend
a party barefoot. With weed,
booze and lopsided caresses. Ideas
propagate. Unrestrained.
A pioneering spirit has built
a carousel of colourful
huts and tents. Made
a space for bonfires. Landscaped
village streets. Set up
rickety stalls on

Trip Road and in Nepal Street,
and a shed for astro-massage
not far from Deadly Nightshade Road.
A crush of rabbits and gnostically
reared children between
the tents. Of dogs, goats,
painted humans. With
and without trousers. In a non-stop
mutating communal freak-out.
Breath by breath I surface
at my own quiet pace.
Vibrations spread. Only
pure fantasy can transfer
dynamic force from the sea's
friction back to the moon.
Travel dizzily away from the camp
in Thy. Where nothing stops
when it's over. Back
for the last year of school.
Equipped with necessary
firsthand knowledge of
a macro-collective break
on an alien planet.
Where I couldn't really live
more than a week of my life.

Playtime

Among ourselves.
To the music. We float out in a scent
of incense. On mattresses placed in a circle
on the floor. Around lit candles.
Joints. Tea. Cakes baked with
hash. Us among one another.
Filtered in and past. One another.
  And then suddenly:
A backward whirling through the world.
The face that will not... Cannot...
Move... Seeks away
from the other. Out
in a hallway with a mirror.
In order to see. Is it still me?
Look in. Into the mirror's tunnel...
  My face. My unknown face.
In the strange house. In the strange
mirror... It moves. The face.
Elastic.
  Not mine. My mother's. Captivated.
In the mirror. Of my mother's
face... Or do I have a double?
Am I inhabited by other souls?
The mirror covered.
By eyes. Nose. Mouth...
Melts. Someone's
whispering loneliness. The face's
mirror... Lips move.
  Without a scream. Twisted.
A skip. For rubbish. Full
of smiles. Pulled crookedly... My mother's
grimaces. Flee. In
to the others again... Back.
To my friends. Now all
on their knees. Among the cushions
on the mattresses. When I enter.
  The candles on the floor. My friends
sway their bodies. Flutter
a forest of arms. Like banners
in a mist in front of me.

113

You know the day destroys the night
Night divides the day.
Tried to run
Tried to hide
Break on through to the other side.
Veil of mist. Dream banners.
The tones race. Like instruments.
Flash. The tones flash. Oxygen
for the heart... Instruments
made of sounds. Of steel. File of
tones. Scalpel of sounds. Awl.
Sounds of needles. Of stings.
Scorpion sounds. Concentrate
in a burning point.
    Burn a hole.
Break on through to the other side.
Through the skin the sounds. Metallic
swarming. Instruments'
sting-flames attack.
Millions of sounds. Invade.
Fluorescent instruments.
Cut. Sound. Electric.
In a rain on the skin. In incisions
on the skin. Shocks...
Slow flames. Sound
drowns light. Injections
of tones. Glowing instruments.
Prick. Perforate. Torture
the fire-second. Flay the skin.
We chased our pleasures here
Dug our treasures there.
    The heart. Does it dance?
Has it stopped?... Do I feel
my heart? The floor against my head.
Heavy sun. The floor. Searchlights of tones.
Break on through to the other side.
Don't want to hear any more. Cut.
Van Gogh's ear off.
    Silence
at last. Home again.
    The sun. A light-flood of summer.
In through my window. In
through a broken pane.

– Who broke the pane
in my room?
I scream
   more than twenty hours later.
Break on through to the other side.
Light-flood of summer's winter sleep. Ice-blue cold.

Studies of This and That

A man has hanged himself, a basement flat is vacant.
I cover despair's bloodily dried
signature on the wall with white paint,
                              move in
to three raw cold rooms with bed, desk, chair,
with clothes, books, the family's discarded kitchen utensils,
dented pots, scratched pans
                    – and a boyfriend.
With him I party wildly and dance
between damp-stained walls
    or in the *Mole*,
when Steppeulvene and Alrune Rod
set music to acid nights,
when melting colours projected onto
the giant screen flow together
    in a migraine-like psychedelic chaos.
With *Life*'s pictures from the Vietnam War
I paper the walls from floor
to ceiling in the hallway, wash
standing at the kitchen sink, share
a toilet with the building's other residents,
    one of whom smokes cigars there.
My hair I let grow, shake it in the wind,
go about in jeans and alternating
    home-dyed men's thermal undershirts
under the same Icelandic sweater.
Fried potatoes and tinned cod roe
cooked on a gas flame,
    I live on.
Spend the rest of the budget
    on books.
Each week I pass hours in central Copenhagen
in a regular shuttle
between jewel-stores of bookshops new and secondhand
with a leather bag that makes my shoulders
    increasingly skewed.
On an island without time
a rocky spur from the darkness,
    I isolate myself.

116

Consume buckets of tea,
   read, read
Strindberg, Camus, Jung, Dostoyevsky,
   read, read
Hamsun, Stefan Zweig, Simone de Beauvoir, Wilhelm Reich,
   read, read
Marcuse, Richard Wright, Ho Chi Minh, Ivan Malinovski.
Every cell in my brain is alive,
                            as if there were a hope
in the bloody sunrise over the city's rooftops.

Revolution

A spectre is haunting Europe
– and so again on a Thursday evening
    a study group is convened.
Out of our bags in a sparsely furnished room
    we pull the manifesto.
The philosophers have only interpreted the world,
in various ways;
the point, however, is to change it
– says the paragraph
I absorb, eager to learn, so as not
    to be left sitting alone.
The wind of change blows
round the corner, breathing life
into the smallest ember.
No laughter celebrates the moment here.
We discuss how society
can be changed, are bitterly at odds
    about correct praxis.
I am keen to abolish injustice,
turn a page:
    The laws of any society therefore also
develop and change through its internal contradictions.
However, a swarm
    of the same species
may also attack one another,
    dip one another in sulphuric acid.
No one shall dictate what
    is best for me.
The past I can imagine
has also made me think about the future,
my lungs are filled
                with invisible joy.
No one else shall take responsibility for me,
but I think without acting,
    refuse
to throw stones during demonstrations.
Am told as an ominous prophecy
that when the
    imminent
revolution arrives
I will be the first to be shot.

Breaking a Chain

Behind closed eyelids I remove the iron chain,
   the barrier now constitutes an opening.
I'm cold and sweating, take
a deep breath, move
   from one reality to another.
It's what the music I listen to
   is about, *Walk on the Wild Side*.
It's what the books are about
   that are engraved
on the inside of my skull,
Spilt Out Sputtering with Acid
or *The Politics of Experience* and *The Bird of Paradise*.
It's what the life I live is about,
so the oxygen pricks in the blood,
                    chaotically mute.
Cinders rewound to sparks
behind the eyes.
The chain around the monument in the city square
I undo in the dream,
enter a black-and-white picture
   where the light is caught
like sunshine through a sieve.
Leave a familiar world in colour
approach a group in which
I instantly recognise someone,
   the bookseller on Nørregade.
From him I buy my textbooks,
in that black-and-white reality he hands me
a book with naked pages.
   I stare into the void.
Those blank pages wait for the tip of the pen
to scratch like the cat's claw at my arm,
fill a furious path
           towards tomorrow
in a disarming rain of light.

Anatomical Institute

Hours I have spent at the Anatomical Institute
among cut-up preparations
   of human beings in tubs and glass containers.
The anatomy book and the compendium
on the cell and its structure
I push aside now,
light a cigarette,
   each breath an extreme awakening.
Late evening, the time is mine.
There is silence in the building
where I have rented
two minimal rooms, silence in the street
   and the little courtyard.
The sleeping city I listen to,
   the sleeping birds.
The poem begins behind the words,
behind the moon's ice
   in a sudden illumination.
I disappear into the written,
   come into being there,
while everything around loses itself
   like distant echoes.
Words rush, the darkness burns under the skin
   in icy drips.
The paper's magnet captures
shavings of sounds, thought-splinters,
   draws sentences' lightning
out of my pulsating body.
The night, a possible gap to capsize in,
but the words carry me
   dizzy and dream-displaced
above the growing abyss.
Not until the sun shows itself
and the silence howls again,
   does the poem stare at me.
Left alone among formless shadows,
where it clutches out again, death –
with the chance of becoming part
of the Anatomical Institute's collection.

Winter's Tale

On the train a man comes up to me
　and asks
what book I'm reading,
　　　　　　Karen Blixen's *Winter's Tales*.
I am seen
by a shining gaze,
don't seek refuge in the landscape
that sweeps past the compartment window,
so that this gaze will not
　wander off elsewhere.
The book is between him and me,
it can't be used as a shield,
because it suddenly
　binds us together.
A better proposal of marriage I have not known,
　it leaves its imprint on the soul.
He is the one by whom a few days later
I'm kissed under a beech tree's
dizzy green crown
　　　　　on an August evening,
as the sun plummets.
We quiver, making all the leaves
set themselves in motion.
The dreams' seeds
　float
in the warm breeze.
He is the one I later
marry,
a winter's tale of high sun and fathomless frost.

Fire of Poppies

I am the hourglass where the sand
does not lie down to sleep.
I want to rest on a wild current,
listen to the rhythm of your blood,
    the beating of your heart.
I want an embrace
that does not shape the being of the embraced
    after the one who embraces.
Want to believe in
what cannot be destroyed,
    and does not destroy.
I am wing and departure
from a halted life.
The dream of a meeting
    exists,
fire of poppies in a wheatfield.
The dream of attaining
shared memory
    without losing oneself.
I would like to think it is possible,
and perhaps it is, but
    only in a poem?
To begin with, tongue and lips are content
to whisper it
            through a crack in time.

Snowploughs, Icebreakers

Through the panes the frost stares at us.
We live differently side by side
in rooms with doors that lead anarchically
   anywhere.
Lay the table and quench our thirst
with water from a shared jug
   in a house that is not ours,
yet snug enough to warm exhausted souls.
The snow's crystals grow in the silence,
   an invasion of white.
Language must constantly engage
headlong, seek new directions
in order to be heard... Can you hear me?
Not least when we go together
where snowploughs have opened a passable route
before the snow blows thickly, shuts us up again
in homeless dreams,
          each in our impression
of the world around us, as if
it is not an identical world
we take part in... Can I hear you?
Together we find our way through a landscape
   without ever seeing the same thing.
In heavy boots and lined coats
we plod forward on a road whose name
   is covered by snow.
We go hand in hand
wearing leather mitts, talking
about the books we're reading.
Listen in nights covered with stars
   to each other's hearts.
We confuse the bitter with the sweet,
think we are meeting each other,
but are each separately mapping out new continents.
We think we are meeting each other,
but it is probably
      mostly ourselves.
Icebreakers break the ice, open shipping lanes.
We must together light a bonfire in the night,

yet nevertheless disappear
              each into our own death,
lie under the ground
              each on an island of our own,
you on Funen, I on Zealand.
That is the only thing that is definite.

Arrival I

A secret more burning than any sun
   I carry,
until a day when, carefree, we celebrate.
Reality has begun to take the shape
   of heaven.
The arched belly under the dress
speaks its own language.
My father
   leans over my chair, kisses my forehead.
My mother
   throws her arms around me when I reveal
the hidden, but possibly suspected.
The joy of fulfilment
flutters around the table with flowers and guests.
A child
wanted by me, wanted by its father,
wanted by the family,
which does not want
               to disappear.
Or has the child
        sought us out?
The road doesn't end, the dust
rises in a weightless gleam of nebula.
As if the world for one moment
   is eternal,
the joy rises around the table,
butterflies mount up to the heights of dreams.

Letters

As yet the letters have no idea
they belong to a spiritual genre that soon
will have outlived itself
   like the echo of centuries.
I write them in the evening in a house
with radiant heat from the fire in the stove
to guard against looming destruction.
Hours open magically,
   the heart sings.
I write them with the same hope I had
when once in the back garden I buried
a dead bird
      so it would sprout again.
The fire crackles, the fingers' strokes
on the typewriter keys
calm the hunting dog by the log basket.
I address the words to the one who will read them,
   no one else.
Present alone with this other,
   only a heartbeat away.
I write the address, weigh the letter
on a wobbly, inherited three-legged scales,
lick stamps,
   because a drop of sender's saliva
will be sent too,
and the taste of glue on the tongue
is an indispensable part
   of the correspondence.
The winter storm settles,
the postman brings back greetings, language
for a common destiny is stored
in the memory
while the brain's catapult
           fires off new thoughts.
Flocks of birds over the roof
   fly south
with the same rush as when the next letter begins.

The Salamander Soul's Dream

Glass captures the rays of the sun, leaps
brittle and fragile,
melts paradise-black, flows
and proliferates in the unpredictable shapes
   of seconds.
Milk-white thoughts' heaving sea of ice,
the sun, the blood,
   time's labyrinth.
Deep-frozen characters dry up,
like a spine
   grow straight,
as tendons and muscles vibrate
tense vortex upon vortex,
   are roused to life
                  by the fire's experiment.
Words seethe and wake
in flames, are constructed
                  in flames,
glow red
in the passage from something to something else.
To die in order to live
forgetting self, put spinal cord colours
into play
      in spring-clear light,
the fear-pulse's seraphic beat.
The salamander soul's dream:
   to lend its light to all.
Salamander sun:
   a life-giving and merciless encounter.

127

Wedge

Your eyes ask me to defend
views I do not share,
expect my lips
to form words,
that are not mine –
    and therefore a lie.
You call it solidarity,
 I call it tyranny.
The Falklands war drives its wedge
in between you and me,
who love each other, but now
 in a single blow are split
and lay a house in ruins.
In the garden the trees cease
their movement, I stop talking and see
your gaze die
 without forgiveness.
The wedge cleaves my thirtieth birthday
cleaves friendships, cleaves us.
 Forgive us our guilt.
A summer evening becomes winter,
 frost-bite, frost-cracks,
earth's coldness tears at the nose.
The fire that has has given warmth
 devours unexpectedly,
estranged, you turn your back.
I survive by jumping
 from ice floe to ice floe
in a sleepless sea.

Arrival II

Before the nights draw an icy net of silver,
the birds, the roses, the apples in the garden,
   lips against lips.
The body knows more than the mind.
That we yearn becomes the desire
which the autumn's honey-coloured light
   awakens in us,
a forgotten language that is called forth
   only by being spoken again.
That we seek the same place,
move into the same dream
   deciphered by the stars,
becomes the child,
that is to be born –
             wanted, wanted.
It lies close to the heart,
when I hum, when I speak,
   wriggles its weightless answers
in the blinding darkness.
Afterwards:
a forest listens, creatures
stop at the edge of the forest,
   sense that it is near.
That there will soon be more of us
                  to meet.
The heart knows no limit,
it loves the next child like the first.

It's the Time

With only a few books behind us we survey one another,
    while we ourselves are viewed
by previous generations with scorn, scepticism
    or a mildly indulgent gaze.
It's the time when we meet on the streets and cafés
    in Copenhagen,
in pubs, on squares, on plazas,
in flats or rented rooms,
listen to music, look at magazines,
    discuss till the blood boils.
No one has invited us in,
no one has created a space for us,
    we find it ourselves.
For where there are poets, there is a stage,
where there's a stage there's an audience,
where there's an audience the energy arises,
    the dynamism and the drama.
We are antennas, capture
    the present's signals.
Invisibly we have looked for one another,
sought both challenge and understanding.
We must put our knowledge together,
but each write from our own place,
                            lift each other up
– that is *my* dream.
Write,
not to save the world,
                but wake it from its torpor
with language in precise karate chops.
It's the time when we turn on the radio, listen
to one another, write letters, call,
meet in galleries, at parties, at readings
at home or on the road,
sometimes bringing trophies
    from hell's antechamber.
Moments of enchantment
where black crystals glow
                    fever-white,
and all refuse to compromise.
The time when some insist
on programme poems and manifestos, others don't,

where some plan performances
in the nearest supermarket, others
    refuse to take part.
The time when men are placed in focus while women
    are sent out to the periphery.
The time when some are admired, others are ignored,
and critics in a true cruelty to animals
    each bet on their own lame horse,
while we as crown witnesses
to each other's triumphs or deafening defeats
try to hold the pen firmly and supply in our hand,
    while our tongue sings in our mouth.
The time that begins in innocence,
but when the men with fatal outcome
inwardly fight to draw the decade
    on a burning blue planet.
Some have opted for tea and coffee,
others for booze and fun substances
    all for a flowering chaos,
poems that breed and breed.
No one now puts another's books back
    unread
on a shelf in the bookcase.
It's the time when it's not being sensed
that outsiders are becoming mainstream,
that we look like a parody of ourselves,
that the next generation
            has begun to sharpen weapons
for both parricide and matricide.
Where will the wind
    blow from tomorrow?
New times, new environments, where there are
loud whispers that distance has replaced thirst for life,
    the safe the rough.
We are seen as the generation who recklessly
use any means
    to test new laws of gravity,
to set an unseen spring loose
                in poetry.
It is the time when angels swim,
    like dolphins frolicking in the sun.
We meet, we build a space, we separate –
floating free
        and each on our own.

Zinnsgade Copenhagen

Too tired to sleep, too awake
   to close an eye.
The sound of car tyres
over wet asphalt,
voices pulverise,
      no axis, no centre.
Unease is nailed to every cell at once,
   the silence is assailed.
In a pause in time I live
with spiral stairs down
to centuries of wisdom earlier
in thirst that this present moment
should cast light into the deaf darkness.
Of this sealed night
there are only a few hours left.
Of this millennium – fifteen years.
Snippets of words hum,
a jumble of constellations
   flaps towards me.
The smallest letter-splinters
in large swarms. Hypothetical drafts…
Do I leave my body?…
Word-flames… Sentence-fire…
Or do I speak in a limbo
with my own shadow?
Do I hope my way through the night,
do I navigate towards a future
or do I capsize
   with burns in my soul?
Throw away what I have in my hands,
rush off, down the stairs
from the attic, out to the street.
Fill breathless lungs
with searing cold air.
   Blood-taste. Blood-mute mouth.
A man with a dog on a leash, him
I catch hold of so as not to vanish
with the speed of flying lightning
   into the side streets of the mind.

The Boy's Excursion

The Chernobyl wind hasn't reached the garden,
when he gets off the train, my seven year-old son
   with backpack
     and the sea in his eyes.
Alights in cold sun
  and frost
    over the forest.
The sea is still burning
          the moment's annual rings.

Glasnost

In the year when Mathias Rust opens the sky and lands
his Cessna 172 on Red Square,
I begin a journey
          on another continent,
which admittedly is accessible, but not explored
    in the farthest corners.
Yes, I have a driving licence. Yes, I can carry
heavy suitcases of photo equipment.
Yes, I only need a few hours of sleep,
I meet all the criteria in the advert
    inserted in the authors' journal.
With no certificate other
    than the blood's rolling under my skin
        and the desire for a lift,
in New York I get into a car
    beside a foreign Viking.
He sits at the wheel, though I can drive,
he carries the heavy suitcases, gives me
– so that I'll be just a little sociable –
permission to sleep every morning
long as a baby.
...the 18 year-old West German changes route
    under the guise of
refuelling in Finland on the way up to Stockholm,
before implementing *his* form of glasnost
    by landing in the middle of Moscow,
getting out and smiling to the astonished Muscovites,
    who smile back to the pilot.
I get access to the heart of the USA,
    to slums and shacks, to bitter brutality,
that not many voluntarily visit.
Drive through a shadow-coloured world
which in every fibre of my nerves
    I must know
in order to continue an imaginary bridge –
sprung from the roots of light-fans deep in the brain
    and with hope at its zenith.

Revolver

– Do I have a soul?
 asks my youngest son,
   in his revolver game
tumbling into the room
   where I sit in thoughts
that tower to treetop height.
– I hope so,
I reply and look up.
– I have one too,
he says.
– Mine will live on when I'm dead,
he continues, already on his way back out
in the autumn that is growing
   over the mushrooms.
Clusters of Trooping Funnel among wet
leaves under November-grey clouds,
behind which a white-yellow glow
shows faintly between the trees,
where the air is raw,
   and my breath
keeps making new misty flowers in the air.

The Fall of the Wall

Wish in January 1989 as strongly
as a person can wish,
that one day I will witness
                    the fall of the Berlin Wall.
Stand 200 years after the French Revolution
in the cold on a high point,
survey concrete, barbed wire and electric fences,
rows of grim, grey barracks.
Wild rabbits hop around in the zone
    between East and West.
In the same year the border is opened,
I watch it time-delayed on the ninth of November
from West End Avenue on American TV.
Guards raise border barriers,
allow unimpeded
cars and pedestrians to move freely
    from East to West,
while people somewhere between day and night dream
                            climb the Wall.
The socialist night is let loose
in the capitalist one, the cheering
    is endless,
the party in the streets lasts all night.
Hear two days later in The Kitchen
Heiner Müller and Heiner Goebbels
perform an encore
                about the fall of the Wall,
the hall seethes, acute joy
    explodes the moment.
The Wall falls, concrete, barbed wire
    and daily fear.
I hear greetings from Germany
in New York,
hear them announced by Heiner Müller,
while he is known as an artist,
    not an agent.
The sun's eye of fire,
something is flowing through time,
the sky grows great above Berlin.

He Learns the Alphabet

When I wake up and my youngest son
    is hanging up in the air,
where I can no longer reach him,
I realise it's my own fault
    that the alphabet divides us.
Letter by letter
            I have followed him on his way,
word by word he rose
with butterfly dust on his shoulders,
    became both bigger and very light.
Yet my son is doing best there
at a language's safe distance
    from his mother.
The world is his,
                emerald green –
I see him rise higher in the light,
try to shout to him in the space
    which is endless
that it is a pleasure to float above the trees.

Departure

Under fallen leaves small creatures look
   for stars,
trickling beings in a rotten storeroom,
when I dig deeper.
A moment of nothing
                before the storm-trees sway.
The forest smells of damp and decay,
an unknown grave swarms
                  with homeless life.
The sun seeps down along the trunks,
insects rustle under dry-rotten bark,
   stagger drunkenly out along a branch.
Cyclone of changes,
no different than a circle of friends struck
by a typhoon's force:
divorces, illness, sudden death.
A society goes under, another rises,
new air flows cool and clear. Breathe. Survive.
Creatures dash up along trunks
disappear into a treetop, where birds
now and then short circuit in song
                       or plummet.
Drops of dreamt light between twigs
or patchy blindness
as after shooting stars on the sky's vault,
before the unavoidable departure
                takes place.

Futile Prayer

May the fields, the woods and the trees in the garden
    always be there,
the delicate pink, strongly fragrant rosebush by the steps
and the overpoweringly thunder-red roses in the garden.
May the row of apple trees and the pear trees on the espalier
    still abound in fruit,
the strawberry plants and thornless brambles
give abundant quantities of berries,
the hedgerow nuts and cherry plums.
May the house filled with whispering memories
    always be there,
the orange-striped cats like ball lightning in the grass, the dog
    in chase of every dream
– that's how one part of the brain thinks
the other has long ago
sent the removal van off
                    to Rosenvængets Sidealle,
is already planning
where the children will sleep, the writing desk stand, the bread be bought,
    not to mention:
What is to be given as answer to a loss.

139

War and Love

Arms race, peace treaty, new aggression
It doesn't take more than two
    to ignite a lightning bolt or start a war.
You have designs on me,
    or is it the other way round?
Two who embrace each other
live not only
            with the kiss's force of gravity.
From my I I can't see into yours
and from your place you can't see into me,
that is what we have in common,
    the only thing we have in common.
In the morning I wake,
you wake, fever-red sun,
    it's not a we that wakes.
You seek closeness with strangers,
    I seek it with you,
can't possibly agree with your ideas,
just as you can't reconcile yourself
with my conceptions, the ones
    I myself may hardly have perceived.
Where you see an entrance, I see
    only a barrier.
Spiritual caltrops
    I sprinkle liberally.
For fear of losing myself
I don't follow your plan.
For fear of vanishing
in fear's labyrinths,
    I detest plans.
In the middle of the kiss's sweetness
                            an alarm goes off.
The sky is black with snow,
    even in peacetime
we take each other's souls.

Resting Pulse

I sit on a freshly painted bench,
alone amidst the fiery green's
mutating silence,
    wait for what
may arise from chaos,
    watch the rain come.
The first drops fall
into the cup of coffee
I have sat down to drink out here,
where the world is drowned out by tall trees
immersed in morning prayer.
I wait for chance to find me,
    plant a design,
so that the shapelessness will acquire form,
colours gain radiance again.
I drink the sound of rain,
listening to the trees' pulse –
the silence is greater than the space.
The rain increases, the nakedness.
Against the soles of my feet the grass
is still sun-warm, underground
odours overwhelm me as they greet me.
A hidden conversation
                is carried on.
Even before I have arrived
    before eye meets eye,
I lean
    like a survivor
against a foreign shoulder.
If the words don't seek shelter
in a poem now, they will get soaking wet.

Melancholy Happiness

The light disappears with the bird-voices,
                                    crushing.
I drag myself down to the sea in the dark.
The tool for transformation has broken down,
first it must be repaired, then I will
explore possible changes,
    then the world will...
Descent. Stand at the water's edge in rubber boots,
waves fall and fall, wash
over my feet, leave
    a little salty foam in the sand.
Stand bent over my soul,
light with a lamp
    towards the bottom.
Have long worried about worries
that make bones crumble,
    infinity
dissolve in the smallest intervals.
The waves beat their numbing blow,
                                    still-water time,
a ringing in my head, a roar.
I'm alive, each cell in my body is alive:
Inhale the brisk sea air. In my lungs
                            the world renews itself.
The sand, the water and the sky are there,
    the cold around my feet.
The water in constant motion here where I stand –
perhaps I should rise with the wave,
    then sink,
rise again, let myself be caught by the wind,
    lifted
between falling stars.
I find myself in the midst of darkness,
shake the worries from me,
    down into the sea.
Will try to muster soul and skeleton,
walk back erect by the flashlight's gleam.

Why Is This a Human Being?

The creature walks on two legs and can use a star screwdriver,
    it laughs and cries loudly.
It consumes food, sleeps, but also speaks and sings,
philosophises and learns Spanish in its spare time or studies
    a drop of its own blood under the microscope.
It sends letters, a weighty proof
    of its human existence,
like the singing of the Christmas carols it has learned
    by heart,
and its mastery of the twenty times table,
    even when it is woken up in the middle of the night.
The lion meets this creation on an open plain,
sees the two eyes, the two ears,
    and the missing fur.
It's the lion
        who wins –
what remains is the human's name.
It is chiselled in the silence on a stone
that plants climb up,
while worms, ants and insects swarm around.
A screaming bird also sometimes lands on it.
The bird isn't sad,
only the people who stop beside the stone.

Unlike the Animals

Unlike the animals, I can name
formations of stars that wind
across the sky:
the Eagle, the Dolphin, the Fox and the Swan,
but the piece of meat we share,
the cat and I,
   it smells tender and sweet;
our teeth gleam and our mouths
   both water.
I consume the largest and juiciest hunk,
while the cat devours the bloody bit
   where shreds hang thick along the cartilage.
Side by side we are thrown a few hours' sleep,
fill our lungs with the same air,
just as we compete
   in enjoying the sun's rays.
The birds' shadows we both pick up,
   enigmatic signs, on the other hand,
I understand just little as my cat,
yet all the same they stimulate
   my thoughts.
I get up after my nap, the cat
makes the leap from the second floor
                    and survives.
I don't think I would have,
but the mind's repeated bungee jumps
are part of the daily repertoire
and the impossible leap
            into an unknown future
I make instinctively.
I turn my face towards a stranger's gaze
   lit
under the infinity of the Bull, the Lion and the Great Bear.

Outside Edge

Dream that a man in a doorway
is watching me.
I recognise him at once,
   am drawn to him.
Or is he looking for me? The gaze penetrates.
   Tiger will, tiger thirst,
the pulse's desire behind a grille of flames.
In the dream the walls lean over me,
the wallpaper in the room is shrivelled,
   there is no window.
A chlorine-white morning light
from the real window
splits the silence
   sickeningly fast.
I am awake and long
   for precisely that gaze
to meet me again, its lightning flash
   sprout
outside the dream.
A luminous wind travels
through a still-green autumn tree.

New Atlas

I know my country, its snowfalls and downpours,
its grey-white sky, the smell
of a newly-turned furrow and the trees,
   when they are lit by sun,
but the eye also captures distant wars
in its black centre,
the ear listens to the accents of fear,
   the same in every language,
so now, when a millennium is about to disappear,
the old atlas must
very probably
     be replaced by a new one.
My thoughts consider before and after,
but the body does not detect this shift,
as always, it longs
         for acute present tense.
Some carry fallen and wounded into the houses,
others declare themselves the winners,
draw new boundary lines, scars on the earth,
which still smells of earth,
  and which reportedly was created
             in a single breath.
I live in the unprotected,
do not have keys to other rooms.
My chest rises and falls, I inhale
the smell of another body, am embraced by it
heart to heart
    without perishing
under a sky expanded by the colours in a cry.

In Another's Mirror

In his morning mirror
I will consider myself,
   not in mine.
In his mirror
to my amazement I
   like myself.
– You ought to have
a mirror like this at home,
   he says.

Transformation Fever

I can decide whether life will stop here,
    as a dream is interrupted,
or tensely start from somewhere else,
wait for the thundershower to clear
the air electrically,
    so I can breathe freely again.
An instinctive hope
    makes me choose the latter.
Two collapsing towers in New York offer this autumn
    as a fixed point.
Why should I not be able to transform myself
when bullet holes, in cities I have visited,
    are covered up with mortar,
when houses reduced to ruins are replaced by new housing,
when within a few years an entire neighbourhood shoots up
where everything lay
                in blood, debris and sorrow.
I have seen it happen.
Although I can't have more children
surely the magic isn't
            over?
Language has many words for loss and resignation
    but doesn't stop.
It loses individual words no one remembers to use,
but stays alive, goes on the prowl in other languages,
    breeds ruttishly and without shame
grows as a wild zone grows,
    hisses, spits
new meanings out, fuck talk, poetry, other variants
    surprising, unruly offspring –
transforms itself inquiringly, becomes new buildings,
new spaces to move into
              with echoes of copulating rhythms.

If the Sun Can Wake Up

There you sit measuring a sarcophagus
with a spirit level,
a colour-blind earth-smell surges, bitter, out.
The sparks I knew
by their long leaps
   drown in the ashes.
The bone gleams dull and burnt-out,
soon the calendar will open
for one long break,
           plenty of time
for endless brooding.
You can brush the dust off your jacket
and roll up the gauze.
With long strips of it
you closed the streets and waved the city
   goodbye,
waved me
   goodbye
– without, however, disappearing.
Your life's Ariadne thread
has branched into a spider web's
floating strands.
You can follow its routes, they all
lead back to a dark womb,
           to the egg's zero.
It's a summer of drought,
you can see your wishing well
silting up,
over and over again count the dead,
until the eddies spin backwards in your brain,
and you snow yourself
   in.
But I want
you to be met beforehand
by a swarm of dreams
and there, deep in the labyrinth,
           be revived
by long-denied instincts.
If the sun can wake up every day, surely you can, too?

Unlike Man

He's crying, to my surprise.
Stands in front of me with tears that fill
Copenhagen's Central Station.
Outside it's raw and foggy,
   a shadowless day.
I shiver in my coat,
philosophise in the crowd about my destiny.
No ray of comfort.
He's crying, so he is
   not an animal,
man can be
both superhuman and inhuman.
An animal, on the other hand,
can only be an animal,
it doesn't dream
        of being loved,
it neither hopes nor remembers.
I remember film seen backwards.
The one who was stabbed with a knife,
quick as a wing,
        got up again unscathed.
Pigeons in the sky's grey colours
flap underneath the dome, land
on the tiles around us.
   Footsteps, wing-beats.
Altered train times are announced,
the world is an inevitable result of language.
Arrivals. Delays. Cancelled departures.
I shiver in my coat.

Closing

In memory of Per Højholt

How to close a poem
was the theme
          of the first conversation
with a senior colleague.
I had only just published
    my debut poem
before the conversation got going.
I listened to a poet
who over the years had closed
so many doors to his poems
that he knew exactly whether they contained
one word too many or too few.
A poem has its own ending built in
and points
        beyond itself.
The day this poet
    is buried,
a thick ground mist has settled
on the landscape, closing
the earth with him
                emphatically and with floating elegance.

151

Spiral

One after the other death drains,
leaving another soul
   I must accommodate.
Children as always want
to be born on this planet,
just as my steps continue
and may unexpectedly cross another's path,
    cross another's path.
Time gnaws at flesh and bones,
sends blurry clouds into
the eye's field of vision,
removes a few notes
from the registers of voices.
But the inherited language refuses
to dry up, a spring leaps,
    something calls.
Around me an enormous
purple radiance now grows.
The air carries my dreams,
    which a ring of fire
lights around the heart.
Fire and water unite,
    light and darkness.
When the compass needle changes direction
when the salamander shoots
                 through fire,
when a column of fire rises,
and the spirit transformed
produces a world in itself –
ejecting in a split second
    words
that glow like scarred skin
on which a life's caresses are engraved.

Old Children

It is one thing to be a parent to one's children,
   something else
to be a mother to one's mother,
and yet feel guilty
         for not having time
to be there when she needs it,
   but making do
with giving good advice, which she doesn't
take
because she only wants to be allowed
   to be herself.
One day being a child
   and comforted –
the next day managing alone, and now
preferring to lean on the wind
           rather than use a walking stick,
rather be blown down
      than buy a walking aid,
rather stay indoors
     than carry an alarm,
rather one day fall
      downstairs
  and die.
Rather die
    than be saved
      and see her family again
and therefore be ready to live a few years more.

Yellow Tulips

The last remnants of black snow have melted away,
so that the pure snow
                    will be remembered again.
Clouds close the spring sky, the morning
gathers the greyness in an avenue of leafless trees
down which all living things must pass -
dogs and their humans
a school break's breathless children.
Sidewalks and streets gleam shiny
after the night's rain
    I let fall on my tongue.
Yellow tulips I will buy.
I have left behind a shattered dream
and crash-landed in a spring.
The day is one hour longer here,
the temperature higher than at home,
but still not much greater
    than in a refrigerator.
A pigeon on a wet roof affectionately
attacks her mate
with beak and claws,
                    beatings of wings.
Just beneath the cold the warmth is waiting,
and in the café on my street
the hearing is sharpened to ragged tones
    from a clarinet,
walls are melting,
            it is never too late.
Yellow tulips are yellow tulips,
when they shine to another in greeting
so there is fire to put out, volcanic innocence.

Helicopter

Forgive, that my throat grew tight,
that tears sprang at the spectacle
of a mistreated animal on TV,
when I could mourn named beings
   who lose their lives.
The sound of the engine approaches
long before the aircraft.
Now a low-flying helicopter is manoeuvring again
above the roof of my apartment building,
   perhaps with a wounded
or dead soldier
   brought home from war
on the way to Copenhagen University Hospital,
perhaps into the history books
               with room for many dead.
With each flight over the house
I try
beneath the whipping rotor blades in the air
to console myself:
       it *may* well be
           a woman in childbirth.
Tears do not fall logically,
and the magpies build
   without cease
a nest in the plane tree in the courtyard to the sound
             of the helicopter,
lose a twig from their beaks,
   fetch a new one again,
      for the sun-bright continuation of the greenness.

Earth-Mute Cry

The nights are without sleep, just a space
to get lost in, stumble in
   alone on the stairs.
My mother is pursued by herself
   in her own home,
does not feel welcome there.
Confusion's sand blows
in all directions, settles
   in every corner.
That which is too big easily
flies away, small things weigh
like immovable stones
            from the pain mountain.
Tears there are no more of,
only dry sighs are released.
The blood flees in vain
from the fugitive. The sweat
   leaps.
If the sorrow grew
like a crop in the field
with roots of deep lightning,
it would be harvested now,
   anguish-grey,
as it already stands and leans.
The fall is there
          so we can get back up again,
but that my mother does not understand.

Host to a Landscape

The steep mountains lift my feet
  up
step by step.
Blue sky, whose dizziness
  falls into me.
The lungs full
  of blue sky.
The eyes full
  of pine trees,
and other wind-resistant vegetation.
The ears full
  of trickling rice-grains'
silence,
  shattered
by a bird's sudden song.
The cheek receives in a stroke
chill and knife-sharp
  silken wind.
The wind filters the hair
  to a nest
for mice or birds.
I throw my sun
over China's Yellow Mountains,
which a moment ago
lay there like primordial formations,
  but are now my guests
and higher up also a flock of children,
whose laughter rolls like avalanches
  down
the steep rock faces.
There is only
  one life
and a myriad of attempts
at growing accustomed
  to the death
that is not far
  from birth.

Seven Dresses for Visibility

I am sewing a dress that can be worn
proudly by one who is born with
an expectant spark in the heart's vessels,
it will perfectly fit large and small,
is spun strong by the bow of the rain
it can be enjoyed a whole life long,
if the cloth is looked after well.

I am sewing a dress that can be worn
silently by new victims of fear,
it can fit large and small,
does not hide vulnerability
as droves of birds are hunted
out of the tree's dense crown,
the fabric flutters in the wind.

I am sewing a dress that can be worn
lightly by new victims of hate,
it is coloured red by blood
and has thunder-black borders,
it can fit large and small,
those who least of all will think
that one should change before the night.

I am sewing a dress that can be worn
by the victims of a cold cynicism
it can fit large and small,
its crazy fabric is made
of fire no downpour will quench,
it will be a reminder that the earth
may open up at any time at all.

I am sewing a dress that can cover
dried blood on the victims of death,
it can hide large and small,
it is shaped by the deep furrows
of tears across the cheek,
the cloth matches the walls of the dark,
the peace in each grave on the planet.

I am sewing a dress that can be worn
in a misty haze of sorrow's
victims, designed for relatives
and friends of the deceased,
it can fit large and small,
anger's first light is visible
between lead-grey threads of pain.

I am sewing the dress that can be worn
securely by one who knows hope,
woven in are the laughter of friends,
quiet tears of joy, the desire
to wake up in spite
of life the disaster took
– it reflects the rays of the sun.

NOTES

THE MIGRANT BIRD'S COMPASS

The Road Is Alive (26)
Hærvejen, the subject of the poem, is the old military road that stretches from Viborg in Northern Jutland and links Southern Jutland with Northern Germany.

SALAMANDER SUN

Game of Dice (100)
A greeting to Mallarmé for *Un coup de dés jamais n'abolira l'hasard*.

Playtime (113)
You know the day, etc: the lines are quoted from *Break On Through*, by The Doors.

Breaking a Chain (119)
Walk on the Wild Side, from Lou Reed's solo album *Transformer*. The two book titles are Johannes L. Madsen's *Spilt Out Sputtering with Acid* and Ronald D. Laing's *The Politics of Experience* and *The Paradise Bird*.

Revolver (135)
First published in *Trappe Tusind* 1 (October 2008). Here in an altered version.

Seven Dresses for Visibility (158)
First published in *Politiken*, 27/7 2011. English translation in *World Literature Today*, August 2011 (http://www.ou.edu/wlt/web-exclusives/poetry-tafdrup-oslo.html) and *Nordic Voices in Translation* (http://nordicvoices.blogspot.com).